The Skilled Pastor

COUNSELING AS THE PRACTICE OF THEOLOGY

CHARLES W. TAYLOR

FORTRESS PRESS
Minneapolis

THE SKILLED PASTOR
Counseling as the Practice of Theology

All Scripture quotations are from the New Revised Standard Version Bible, copyright © 1989 by the Division of Christian Education of the National Council of the Churches of Christ in the United States.

Interior design: Publishers' WorkGroup
Cover design: Spangler Design Team

Library of Congress Cataloging-in-Publication Data

Taylor, Charles W., 1937–
    The skilled pastor : counseling as the practice of theology /
Charles W. Taylor.
        p.   cm.
    Includes bibliographical references.
    ISBN 0-8006-2509-9 (alk. paper)
    1. Pastoral theology.   2. Pastoral counseling.   I. Title.
BV4011.T38   1991
253.5—dc20
                                                                            91-13455
                                                                            CIP

The paper used in this publication meets the minimum requirements of American National Standard for Information Sciences—Permanence of Paper for Printed Library Materials, ANSI Z329.48-1984. ∞™

Manufactured in the U.S.A.   AF 1-2509

                                                                20   19   18   17

The Skilled Pastor

To

Fay Helen Phillips Taylor
whose love has inspired me
these past twenty-seven years

Contents

Preface

THIS BOOK INTRODUCES three key aspects of pastoral care and counseling—helping skills, theological assessment, and the use of religious resources—by integrating them into a three-stage pastoral conversation model. This construct is called the metanoia model (*metanoia* is a New Testament Greek word that means "to change one's mind") because it helps people deal with their concerns through changing their perspectives. Because the metanoia model focuses on beliefs as a key factor in the way human beings handle situations, it is able to make good pastoral use of religious resources such as Scripture and Christian teaching, which are designed to influence outlooks. Although pastoral theologians may find the discussions of theological assessment and religious resources illuminating and the combination of nondirective and directive counseling theories fascinating, this model can be understood and practiced by those with no background in theology or psychology. However, this book does not deal with the in-depth counseling that is the vocation of the specialized pastoral counselor. Instead, *The Skilled Pastor* is focused on the everyday pastoral conversations and the very brief counseling that is the regular service of both those who provide care at home and work and the laity, seminarians, clergy, and counselors who minister in a parish.

The helping skills provide the framework of the metanoia model. The importance of these skills in any type of helping conversation has been well documented. Virker (1980) confirms that many ordained pastors are deficient in these skills and need specific training in them. In response to this need, pastors and seminary teachers have turned to a number of nonreligious texts. These texts, however, do not show pastors how to use the skills to identify, correct, and deepen religious beliefs and values—central tasks of ministry.

Although skill training provides the framework of this book, theological assessment is at its core. Understanding persons' concerns theologically is important so pastors can draw upon the wisdom of the Christian heritage in caring for these persons. That is, when a problem is framed in psychological terms, psychological resources spring to mind, and religious resources seem like mere add-ons or escapes. In contrast, when an issue is understood theologically, religious resources seem fundamental to treatment. Furthermore, theological assessment helps one decide which resources to use and how they are to be used.

This book, then, is distinctive in at least three ways. First, this book presents a simple form of theological assessment that can be used by beginners. I have observed that students are more likely to use, and continue using, a simple method than a complex one. Once students experience the relevance of theological assessment through practice, however, they are likely to add more complex methods to their repertoire. Second, this book understands theological issues as the central dynamic in persons' troubles. Crippling guilt, paralyzing anxiety, and destructive anger—these painful emotions, which are powerful components of most problems, are understood to be produced and sustained by clinging to lesser values (idols) as ruling values. Third, the model developed in this book links together helping skills and theological assessment to enable theological assessment to be a normal part of a pastoral interview. Thus theological assessment can be done easily during the course of any conversation.

I have been deeply moved by the positive response that seminary students have given this model as it has been developed, since 1978, in my "Introduction to Pastoral Care" course. I have been impressed, also, with the effectiveness of this model as a way of teaching helping skills, theological assessment, and the use of religious resources to lay pastoral care trainees and clergy in various workshops. But I owe the most to those forty-two brave students* who, on the basis of exposure to the model in the introductory course, volunteered to return and help teach it during the last semester of their seminary careers. On the foundation of their support and encouragement, I offer this volume.

I owe particular thanks to Professors Rosemary Chinnici, Elizabeth Liebert, and Vernon Strempke, colleagues at the Graduate Theological

The forty-two pastoral assistants are: Mary Allen, Sue Auchincloss, William Bennett, Jane Moorhouse Bourcet, Robert Chrisman, John Connell, Ellen Davis (Lewin), Judith Dunlop, Katherine Flarity, Elizabeth Goodyear-Jones, Douglas Gordon, Francis Hebert, Polly Hilsabeck, Beverly Hosea (Ost), Virginia Brown Hunt, Margaret Irwin, Mary Jizmagian, Mary Johnson, Peter Kalunian, JoAnn Zwart Leach, Katherine Lehman, Gale Morris, Michael Munro, Elizabeth Newnam, Kathleen Patton, Jeffrey Paul, David Powell, Brian Prior, Bruce Robison, David Roseberry, Thomas Shaver, Judith Stevens, Kristin Sundquist, Karen Swanson, Lee Teed, Penelope Warren, Sharolyn Welton, Jan West, Carolyn White, Edward Wilson, Jo Ann Wright, and Michael Wyatt.

Union, and Doctors Bonnie Ring and Penelope Warren, former students, each of whom read portions of the manuscript and greatly improved it by their comments.

Special accolades go to Joye Pregnall who helped me with my writing at the start of this project. Honor is due, also, to Margo Delaney and Mary Lynn Sepkowitz, who proofread different drafts of this manuscript. The fourth recipient of these praises is Timothy Staveteig, academic editor at Fortress Press, who guided me through the terrors of my first book.

Any mention of my wife, Fay, that is less than a booklength hymn of thanksgiving verges on damning her with faint praise. Because I have not yet composed that lyric, I dedicate this book to her. This work would never have been written without her gracious and cheerful support. My children, David, Paul, and Joy, helped me in another way: they challenged me to practice what I teach.

Above all, glory, honor, and praise is given to God whose Son our Savior Jesus Christ was lifted high upon the cross that he might draw the whole world to himself. I finish this book on September 14, Holy Cross Day, especially mindful of and thankful for the mystery of our redemption.

Charles W. Taylor

The Skilled Pastor

Becoming a Skilled Pastor

WHAT IS A SKILLED PASTOR? How does a skilled pastor differ from an unskilled one? What are the pastoral skills and how are they used? One way to understand my response to these questions is to compare the following pastoral visits with Martha.

A TYPICAL HOSPITAL VISIT

Martha is forty-three. She and her husband have three healthy, developmentally normal children who are eight, ten, and twelve years old. She has been active in Bethany Church for ten years. At the time of these visits she is in the hospital recuperating from an operation, but she is feeling well enough to have serious conversations.

Jude was at the hospital to see his aunt and dropped by to see Martha. He knew Martha well as they had worked on several church committees together during the eight years that Jude had been active at Bethany. He was a little nervous about what he would say to Martha because he wasn't used to visiting sick persons. Yet he was determined to visit her because he had desperately wanted visitors when he was in the hospital.

The Conversation

Jude opened the conversation by greeting Martha and asking her how she was feeling. Martha responded by complaining about being hospitalized. After Martha finished there was a brief moment of silence, then Jude, sympathizing with Martha, said, "I certainly know what you mean when you say it's tough being hospitalized." He then proceeded to tell Martha in great detail about the various frustrations he had with doctors, nurses, volunteers, and the billing department during his last stay in the hospital. Martha, not wanting to be unpleasant with this person who had been considerate enough to come by, smiled, nodded, and listened until Jude had finished. Then Martha said, "I wonder if my husband is doing all right with the kids. They are a lot to manage." Jude cheerfully responded, "You have nothing to worry about with that fine husband of yours. I know, I watch the way he handles your kids at church. My wife is continually harping on me to treat our kids the way he does yours." Martha replied in a quiet, flat voice, "Maybe you're right." Jude continued with this pep talk about how competent Martha's husband was and how he wished he had such talent with children, exhorting Martha not to worry. When Jude had finished Martha smiled thinly and thanked him for dropping by. The visitor took the cue; after promising to drop in again, he said good-bye and left.

Reflection

After this conversation Martha felt frustrated, guilty, and confused. Martha was frustrated because she didn't feel like she was heard. Jude seemed to be talking more about his own feelings about hospitals and children than responding to Martha's concerns. In addition, Jude's pep talk had intensified the guilt she was already feeling about how much she was worrying about her husband taking care of the kids. Last, Martha was confused about two things: First, she was troubled by her feelings about the visitor; she knew that Jude meant well, yet Martha was glad when he left. Second, she still wasn't sure how to deal with the guilt and anxiety she felt.

Jude left the room relieved because he had found something to talk about with Martha, especially after the conversation almost collapsed into silence. Yet, he wondered how the conversation went. He had tried to cheer Martha up by telling her how fortunate she was to have such a husband—Jude did, in fact, wish he could be as good with children—but he had a sense that Martha had not really been cheered by what he said. Jude wished he knew how to help people feel better by having a conversation with them; he wished he had some outline of the way the conversation should go.

A SKILLFUL HOSPITAL VISIT

Chris has been the pastor of Bethany Church for twelve years. She knew and liked Martha well enough to have appointed Martha head layperson of the church's board two years ago for the year in which Chris took a three-month sabbatical. As head layperson, Martha was in charge of the congregation while Chris was away.

Conversation

Chris opened the conversation with a greeting and then asked Martha how she was feeling. Martha responded by complaining about being hospitalized. Chris drew out Martha's concerns by putting her thoughts and feelings in different words, or paraphrasing. It soon became evident to both of them that Martha's chief issue was worry about her children's welfare during her hospitalization. Her key statement was made with great emotion, "I just don't think my husband can take care of the children the same way that I do, and I know that I shouldn't worry about it so much—but I do."

After Martha said this, Chris probed carefully to see whether Martha was worried because her husband had some pattern of neglect, abuse, or gross incompetence in handling the children. When Martha convinced her that this was not the issue, Chris summarized Martha's concerns by stating, "It seems to me that the most uncomfortable thing about being in the hospital is your constant worry about the children not getting the proper care from your husband. You feel guilty about worrying so much because he does love them and can take care of them. Is that about right?" Martha confirmed Chris's summary.

Then Chris said, "I wonder if you believe that a good Christian must not be anxious?" Martha replied, "Yes, I guess I do. My mother always quoted that Scripture, 'Be ye not anxious,' and I guess it stuck with me that anxiety is wrong."

After putting Martha's statement into different words, Chris asked her what might make her so anxious regarding the children. After some prompting, Martha said, "I keep thinking that it would be a catastrophe if something happened to them, and I wasn't there." Chris then offered another summary that included the beliefs that lay behind Martha's guilt and anxiety.

Then the conversation shifted. Chris addressed Martha's worry and embarrassment by reminding her about how worried Chris had been about leaving the parish in Martha's care during Chris's sabbatical. Chris then asked Martha if she remembered her own advice. After a pause, Martha smiled and replied, "I told you that you needed to learn to trust us and that you needed to turn the parish over to God in prayer."

Martha's smile got broader and she continued, "You certainly play dirty, reminding me of what I said." They then had a good laugh together. The laughter helped Martha feel less guilty and anxious. It freed her to decide that she wanted to stop worrying so much about the children.

Again, the conversation changed when Martha asked Chris, "What enabled you to stop bugging me after I gave you the advice to turn it over?

How did you turn the parish over to God?" Chris answered, "I worked out this plan to pray for you and the church board for fifteen minutes at the beginning of each day. After a week or so of doing this, I calmed down." Martha thought about this answer for awhile and decided to pray for her children and husband whenever she woke up, either in the morning or during the day. At Chris's suggestion, she agreed to keep a record of this praying so that they could discuss it during her next visit.

Then Chris urged Martha to review the plan; when she did this accurately, Chris realized that Martha was ready to implement it. They prayed together with Chris acknowledging Martha's anxiety and guilt before God and then putting these feelings in the context of scriptural images of God's power and forgiveness. Then Chris said good-bye and left.

Reflection

Martha felt much better after Chris's visit; her feelings had been taken seriously and responded to helpfully. She was especially glad to be reminded that Chris had similar feelings about leaving her parishioners as Martha had about leaving the children. Martha realized that being worried was not so un-Christian after all. Chris's mention of her fear and guilt in prayer had seemed strange at first, but then Martha felt relieved to verbalize it before God. Another benefit of the conversation was the plan for dealing with her uncomfortable feelings.

Chris also felt good when she left the room. She really enjoyed helping people work through their concerns. It was especially rewarding for Chris to be able to come to the aid of Martha, who had assisted her on many occasions. Chris reflected on how much better her pastoral conversations were when she disciplined herself to adhere to the three-stage model.

DEFINITIONS

Chris is an example of a skilled pastor and Jude is an unskilled pastor. The difference is this: Chris is adept at using helping skills, theological assessment, and religious resources to communicate the gospel to parishioners, whereas Jude is not. In order to discuss this difference, key terms need to be defined.

Pastor

I use the term *pastor* to refer to both lay (Jude) and ordained persons (Chris) who fulfill their baptismal vocation by attempting to communicate the gospel through interpersonal relationships. Thus, the term applies to: Christian parents who attempt to talk with their children in ways that communicate both their and God's love; Christian businesspeople who respond to their associates and customers in ways that are helpful and witness to God's love; lay ministers who visit the sick, lead groups, serve on committees, teach classes; seminarians who are taking courses in pastoral care and counseling; and ordained persons who counsel persons in crises such as sickness and grief, as well as in joys such as preparation for marriage and baptism.

Parishioner

Just as the term *pastor* refers to both lay and ordained persons, *parishioner* refers to any person who is receiving pastoral care. I prefer the term *parishioner* over counselee, client, helpee, or patient because it is a term reserved for discussions of pastoral care; the other terms have extensive usage outside the pastoral context. Thus, depending on one's particular ministry, parishioner can be replaced with teenager or business associate or classmate or daughter. This book focuses on the ministry of one-to-one pastoral care, but the skills can be used in the care of couples, families, and committees and other small groups.

Communicate

To *communicate* is to make known or to impart. Communication between pastors and parishioners takes place on at least four levels at the same time: verbal, nonverbal, dynamic, and symbolic. The *verbal* level refers to the words we use. Facial expressions, posture, gestures, and tone of voice are key aspects of the *nonverbal* level. The *dynamic* level points to the interaction between persons. The *symbolic* level refers to the meaning conveyed by the attire, ritual actions, roles, and environment of the participants. In helping conversations, nonverbal, dynamic, and symbolic levels of communication are more powerful than verbal levels. Therefore, effective communication of the gospel in pastoral relationships needs to include the nonverbal, dynamic, and symbolic levels.

The Gospel

The *gospel* is the good news that God is with us and for us. This good news is most fully conveyed through the birth, life, teaching, death, and resurrection of Jesus Christ. Pastors as members of Christ's body, the church, are witnesses to his death and resurrection. Because of Christ's redeeming work, pastors can proclaim forgiveness to the guilty, hope to the anxious, and reconciliation to the alienated. The communication of this good news is the central activity of pastoral care.

Chris communicated the gospel to Martha through deed and word. As a representative of God and the church, she conveyed God's presence and love by being present to Martha through active listening (nonverbal and dynamic levels), and by sharing her similar struggles—using her symbolic role in a way that made Martha feel accepted. Chris also expressed the gospel in words during the final prayer (verbal); those words had power for Martha partly because of the good quality of her interaction with Chris.

In contrast, Jude did not communicate the good news as well. His unskilled listening and premature sharing (dynamic level) conveyed absence rather than presence, self-absorption instead of caring. Thus his verbal attempt at cheering Martha up was perceived as bad news. Even if he had tried to pray with Martha at the end of the conversation, the religious words would have lost much of their power and meaning because of this poor interaction.

Helping Skills

Helping skills are pastors' ways of listening, responding, challenging, and initiating action that have proved most effective in creating good nonverbal, verbal, and dynamic communication. The helping skills presented in this book are based on works by Robert Carkhuff (1969a, 1969b, 1979, 1983) and Gerald Egan (1975, 1982). I have adapted these skills to express and enhance their usefulness in communicating the gospel by illustrating their use in pastoral situations, integrating them with theological assessment, and relating them to religious resources.

The importance of these skills is illustrated by Jude's confusion of his and Martha's complaints about hospitalization, a direct result of Jude not using the responding skill of paraphrasing. By contrast Chris used this skill, and Martha felt that she had been understood and gained insight into her own feelings.

Theological Assessment

Theological assessment is the art of thinking about parishioners' stories from a theological perspective. One of the major reasons that parishioners seek out pastors is to obtain this perspective (Pruyser, 1976). Parishioners want help in understanding the relevance of God to their issues. Thinking theologically about pastoral issues is important for pastors because knowledge of the theological issue helps them to choose the most helpful metaphor, Scripture. prayer, or other religious resource.

The underlying assumption of this book is that the present situation is only one aspect of the parishioner's concern; the parishioner's perspective contributes to his or her difficulty in handling the concern. This assumption is important because often the situation cannot be changed, but the way a person views it can. When things can be changed, one is better able to make useful modifications if one's beliefs are constructive. In Martha's case, the situation (her husband taking care of the children) was not the real cause of her worry. Her belief that it would be a catastrophe if something happened while she was not present was the core of her concern. Although she could not change her being hospitalized away from the children, she could learn a way to practice trusting God.

Given the importance of one's viewpoint in sustaining troublesome feelings or inappropriate behavior, the task of theological assessment is to identify the beliefs that contribute to a parishioner's difficulty. For example, Chris discovered that Martha's guilt was caused by her belief that a good Christian must not worry. Chris then used theological understanding of guilt to formulate a strategy for disarming that belief.

Religious Resources

Religious resources include the church's traditional methods of teaching the gospel's perspective and uprooting unhelpful beliefs. Seven categories of religious resources are generally available for communicating the gospel in pastoral situations:

- The *pastoral person* represents God and the church and is responsible for communicating the good news by word and deed.
- *Scripture* contains the basic statements of the good news by which all others are measured.
- *Christian tradition* provides instructive examples of persons and groups whose lives and teachings illustrate the gospel in various ages, cultures, and situations.
- *Contemporary theology and ethics* proclaim the good news in the language of our time and culture.
- *Covenant communities* are groups of two or more Christians who provide support for living according to the gospel.
- *Prayer* includes those various types of spiritual disciplines, techniques, devotional materials, and arts (poetry, music, drama, visual arts) that support private and corporate awareness of God's presence and love.
- *Rites* are rituals such as Eucharist, Baptism, marriage, and burial that combine the other resources into one powerful multilayered statement of the gospel.

Each of these resources can be an effective means of correcting unhelpful beliefs and strengthening the gospel perspective. In every pastoral conversation, however, the religious resource most at hand is the pastoral person. Chris used her own experience as an extension of that basic resource. She also used prayer in two ways: she used it at the end of the conversation as a way of overtly putting the conversation in the context of God's presence and power, and she offered Martha a discipline of praying that could help her deal with anxiety.

THE METANOIA MODEL

Helping skills, theological assessment, and the religious resources have been integrated into a pastoral conversation form that I call the "metanoia model." The Greek word *metanoia* means to change one's mind or attitude. This term is used to indicate that the focus is helping parishioners change their understandings as a prelude either to coping with a problem situation or to making changes in it.

The three stages in a parishioner's handling of a problem are: (1) exploring, (2) understanding, and (3) acting. These stages are based on the universal human problem-solving process of exploring the situation, understanding what can be done about it, and acting to change oneself, the situation, or both. In exploring (stage 1), parishioners examine where they are by sharing their stories. Pastors use the presence skills (attending, responding, and assessing) to help parishioners identify their underlying feelings and beliefs about their issues. In understanding (stage 2), parishioners realize how their perspectives contribute to the problem and how the good news offers alternatives. Pastors use proclamation skills to challenge unhelpful beliefs and share the good news. In acting (stage 3), parishioners develop and implement a plan to change their beliefs and behavior. Pastors use guidance skills to help parishioners develop effective action plans. Figure 1 gives a summary of the relationship between pastors' skills and parishioners' stages.

FIGURE 1

	Pastor	[enables]	Parishioner
Stages			
1	Presence		Exploring
2	Proclamation		Understanding
3	Guidance		Acting

With this brief introduction to the three stages, pastors are prepared to understand the following analysis of the conversation between Chris and Martha which illustrates the pastor's skills and the parishioner's stages.

Stage 1: Exploring

Parishioner. Martha became more aware of the source and nature of her discomfort with being hospitalized by talking about her feelings, thoughts, and experiences with Chris. Martha became deeply aware of how anxious she was about her children and how guilty she was about this worry. She had not been as clear about what she was experiencing until Chris's active listening drew it out of her. She also became aware of the beliefs that were behind her feelings.

Pastor. Chris helped Martha tell her story by paraphrasing her statements until they both had a sense of what was bothering Martha. This helped Chris to be sure that her understanding of Martha's statements was the same as Martha's. After she had a grasp of Martha's worry about the children and Martha's guilt about that worry, Chris probed to clarify whether or not the amount of Martha's worry was related to the situation. She then offered a summary of her understanding of Martha's feelings and thoughts. Chris could tell by observing Martha's facial expression and listening to her voice cues, as well as her verbal response, that this summary was accurate. After Martha confirmed her summary, Chris then suggested the underlying belief that was sustaining Martha's guilt, with which Martha agreed. Then Chris elicited Martha's reason for being anxious with a question. The pastor concluded this stage by offering a summary that Martha accepted.

Stage 2: Understanding

Parishioner. After Martha had told her story and agreed with Chris's summary, she was ready to hear Chris's perspective (the first turn in the conversation). Martha was afraid that she was going to hear the same moralistic advice, You shouldn't worry, that she had heard from Jude. When she heard Chris witness that Chris had similar anxiety in an analogous situation, Martha felt the good news that she was not alone in being anxious. When Chris asked Martha to remember her own advice, Martha was reconnected to her own wisdom that gave her confidence in her own abilities and in prayer, another element of good news. Martha laughed and accused the pastor of playing dirty, indicating that she had deeply heard the word of acceptance and promise. She was ready to move forward in forgiveness and hope.

Pastor. On the basis of the agreed-upon summary, Chris decided that Martha's primary feeling was anxiety and that her secondary feeling was guilt. Chris knew that the anxiety was sustained by lack of confidence in God and that guilt had to do with feeling alone and unacceptable to God and neighbor. Because of this theological assessment, Chris decided to address Martha's guilt by witnessing to her own participation in similar guilt and to challenge Martha's anxiety by confronting her with her own advice—two effective strategies to challenge perspectives. Chris used her own experience as a religious resource.

Stage 3: Acting

Parishioner. Feeling less guilty about worrying and more hopeful about controlling the worry (the second turn in the conversation), Martha was ready to develop a plan of action. Her goal was to control the worry by turning her children and husband over to God. After listening to Chris's proposal, Martha developed a program of praying for her family every time she woke up. She accepted the pastor's advice that keeping a record of her praying and reporting the results would provide the reinforcement she needed to implement her program. The final prayer brought everything together for Martha, cementing the feelings of acceptance and competence that she had during this conversation and motivating her to deal with her issues.

Pastor. Chris knew that Martha was ready to work out a program when they laughed together; she could tell that a weight had been lifted from Martha's shoulders by the sound of her laughter and the way her whole face lit up. Because Chris knew that goals and programs work best if they come from the parishioner, she checked with Martha to find out what she wanted to do and how she wanted to do it. When asked, Chris was glad to witness to what worked for her but she did not push her own way as the way for Martha. After Martha had decided to undertake a similar program, Chris's job was to help Martha to make it concrete—to decide when, where, how, and with whom she was going to do what. When Martha developed activities and times to do them, the pastor's next responsibility was to help Martha create reinforcements that would support her in carrying out the program. Chris knew that recording one's progress in carrying out a program and reporting that progress to another were two of the most powerful reinforcements, yet they were simple enough for Martha to do in this situation. Chris's final responsibility was to help Martha plan implementation by reviewing her program. With that done, the pastor closed the interview by engaging Martha in prayer as a way of helping her experience the good news of God's presence and power.

MORE THAN A METHOD

This book is designed to aid lay and ordained persons to become skilled pastors—adept at using helping skills, theological assessment, and religious resources to communicate the gospel to parishioners. These pastoral skills are integrated into the three-stage metanoia model that can be used to learn the skills and organize pastoral conversations. This problem-solving or problem management model is designed to respond to the one-time conversations and very brief counseling (up to six weekly sessions that are focused on a specific problem or situation) that characterize the majority of pastoral contacts.

My description of a skilled pastor is not to imply that communicating the gospel is simply learning a few techniques. Methods are not enough: Pastors need both an appropriate understanding of the good news and a passion for sharing it. The use of these pastoral skills, however, can help willing persons deepen their understanding of the good news and strengthen their ability to share it with others. Because all baptized persons are called to proclaim the good news of God in Christ by word and example, all baptized persons have the privilege and responsibility to become skilled pastors. The following chapters introduce means for carrying out that vocation.

Although this book is rightly focused on pastors' skills, the real counselor is the Holy Spirit (John 14:26; 16:12-13), who is teaching the parishioners directly. Pastors learn the helping skills so that they do not quench the Spirit with inept responses, but rather help parishioners to hear and follow the Spirit's teaching. Likewise, theological assessment is crucial for identifying what the Spirit is doing and religious resources are means of strengthening parishioners in the Spirit. Therefore, in spite of this necessary emphasis on the skills of pastors, pastoral conversations are exercises in mutual listening to the Spirit who speaks through each participant for the edification of both. Skilled pastors are not experts who dispense knowledge to the uninformed; they are fellow students who learn more about the gospel through listening and responding to others.

PART ONE

PRESENCE

1

Attending

THE PRESENCE SKILLS (stage 1) are attending, responding, and assessing. These are called presence skills because their purpose is to help pastors be "present to" or "with" parishioners. Achieving *empathy*—understanding things from parishioners' points of view—is their goal. The relationship established by being with parishioners and the understanding gained by seeing things from their perspectives are the bases for any information, insights, or suggested actions that pastors offer. Thus the presence skills are the key helping skills because all the other skills depend on them. Attending, responding, and assessing are the means by which pastors listen to the Holy Spirit speak through parishioners.

The presence skills enable parishioners to engage in their stage 1 task of exploring their problems or joys (see figure 1). The stage 1 set of skills—attending, responding, and assessing—helps parishioners tell their stories in ways that encourage parishioners to recognize, express, and deepen their understandings of their feelings, experiences, actions, and thoughts about their situations. Talking about these things with another relieves parishioners' sense of isolation. When parishioners divulge their stories to a representative of God and the church, they experience the good news that God is with and for them. Pastors facilitate parishioners' exploring by mediating God's presence through the quality of their own presence. Exploring is the way by which parishioners hear anew what the Holy Spirit is saying to them.

THREE SKILLS OF ATTENDING

Three attending skills—positioning, observing, and listening—are the first aspect of being present. *Positioning* is situating our bodies to communicate attentiveness. *Observing* is noticing the messages that parishioners give through nonverbal behaviors. *Listening* is heeding both their words and manner of speaking.

In the same way that the presence skills are the most important of the helping skills, attending is the basis of the presence skills. The nonverbal and verbal data gathered from observing and listening are the material to which pastors react in responding and assessing. Of the two kinds of data, nonverbal data usually reveal more of parishioners' feelings and thoughts than verbal data because most people exercise greater control over their words.

WELCOMING A WIDOWER

Two conversations illustrate the importance of attending. These conversations take place after the Sunday morning service. The parishioner, Mr. Brown, is a recently widowed sixty-two-year-old who has been an active member of the church. Ushers (Mr. Jones and Mr. Gomez) are the pastors in these conversations.

Mr. Jones Greets Mr. Brown

MR. JONES: Good to see you back at church, Mr. Brown. How is it going? [*Said cheerily*]

MR. BROWN: It's going fine. [*Said slowly with his voice tailing off at the end and looking down toward the floor*]

MR. JONES: Well, good to hear it, I guess you can't keep a good man down . . . Right? [*Continues cheeriness*]

MR. BROWN: I guess so. [*Said in the same slow, tailing-off voice, but his focus changes as he looks up and away from the usher and begins to back away*]

Mr. Gomez Greets Mr. Brown

MR. GOMEZ: Good to see you back at church, Mr. Brown. How is it going? [*Said cheerily*]

MR. BROWN: It's going fine. [*Said slowly with his voice tailing off at the end and looking down toward the floor*]

MR. GOMEZ: Sounds like things are pretty rough. [*Said quietly without cheeriness, while focusing on the parishioner*]

MR. BROWN: Yep . . . they are . . . [*He then looks up at the usher*] But I think I'll pull through. [*Said a little louder and quicker*] Thanks for asking. [*The slightest bit of a smile begins to form on his face*]

MR. GOMEZ: So it's hard but you feel good about your chances of pulling through. [*He continues in a quiet but firm voice*]

MR. BROWN: Yeah . . . but I do . . . I wish I had someone to talk about it with. [*Said quietly, while his eyes focused down and to the side*]

MR. GOMEZ: Would you like to go to lunch now and talk about it? [*Continues same manner of speaking and focus*]

MR. BROWN: That would be fine. [*Said strongly, with his head moving up and down*] If it's not too much bother. [*Added perfunctorily*]

Analysis

In the first conversation, Mr. Jones does not respond empathetically either to Mr. Brown's nonverbals (looking down toward the floor) or to his manner of speaking (slowly with his voice tailing off toward the end), both of which disagree with his verbal statement, "It's going fine." Instead, Mr. Jones continues his cheeriness and makes a response that reflects only the parishioner's verbal statement. Mr. Brown responds to the pastor's lack of attentiveness by verbally agreeing but nonverbally disengaging—looking away and backing away.

In the second conversation, Mr. Gomez ignores the verbal response, "It's going fine," and responds to the nonverbals and manner of speaking. The pastor drops his cheeriness and states to Mr. Brown the pain he sees and hears. The parishioner responds by confirming Mr. Gomez's observations and thanking him for noticing. Mr. Gomez continues the conversation by restating Mr. Brown's response, in order to help the parishioner say anything more he needs to say. The parishioner, now deep in his feelings and thoughts (looking down and to the side), reveals or discovers his need to discuss his grief with someone. The pastor responds with a proposal to deal with the need (go to lunch) and Mr. Brown accepts the proposal with his verbal yes being confirmed by his nonverbal actions and his manner of speaking.

Mr. Jones may have missed Mr. Brown's nonverbals and manner of speaking or he may have chosen to ignore them in a premature attempt to cheer Mr. Brown up. In either case, Mr. Jones did not communicate empathy through attentiveness. The result was that Mr. Brown disengaged from him. In contrast, in the second conversation Mr. Gomez communicated his attentiveness and empathy both by his statements and his nonverbal actions. Thus the parishioner became involved enough to admit both his grief and his need to discuss it. These conversations show the importance of attending even in brief conversations.

POSITIONING

Positioning is being physically oriented toward the parishioner. It is the outward and visible sign of an inward and spiritual respect. Positioning, like participating in other sacramental activities, both expresses and nurtures this inward condition. As with all symbols, the form and meaning of positioning is determined by both the culture and the relationship of the pastor and the parishioner. The following five aspects of positioning are especially effective with middle-class North Americans and others who are comfortable with their culture.

Egan (1982b, 60–61) makes the five aspects of positioning memorable with the acronym *SOLER*. They are:

S   face the [parishioner] Squarely
O   adopt an Open position (uncrossed arms and legs)
L   . . . it is possible at times to Lean toward the [parishioner]
E   maintain good Eye contact
R   try to be relatively Relaxed while engaged in these behaviors

These guidelines should not be practiced in a rigid fashion. People differ both individually and culturally as to how they communicate concern for others. For instance, some upper-middle-class persons maintain that no well-bred woman sits in a skirt or dress with uncrossed ankles. Women who cross their ankles communicate dignity and trustworthiness to those who respect this style, whereas those who do not respect such a practice can be put off by this behavior.

Some controversy also exists about leaning toward parishioners. Egan suggests it as a possibility to be considered, but Carkhuff (1979, 41) makes it a standard: "When seated [the helper] should lean forward about 30 degrees until [the helper] can comfortably rest his [or her] forearms on his [or her] thighs. When standing, [the helper] should incline his [or her] upper body about 10 degrees forward—not enough to appear uncomfortable but enough to say, in effect, 'I am inclined to help you.' " Egan (1982b, 61) is concerned that "leaning too far forward or doing so too soon may frighten a client. It can be seen as a way of demanding some kind of closeness or intimacy." Both Egan and Carkhuff agree that leaning back or slouching generally communicates a lack of interest. As with the other four aspects of positioning, the pastor needs to adopt a style that is comfortable for her or him while at the same time being sensitive to parishioners' responses to it.

The five aspects of positioning can serve as criteria for evaluating both parishioners' and pastors' involvement in various parts of a pastoral conversation. When parishioners who began the conversation slouched in their chairs lean forward, they likely have become more involved in the conversation. Similarly, when a pastor repeatedly folds his or her arms and leans back during a pastoral conversation, the pastor is likely withdrawing from the conversation.

In addition to drawing parishioners into conversations and serving as criteria for involvement, these five aspects of positioning have a third function: facilitation of *observing*. Facing parishioners squarely, with steady eye contact, and being relatively relaxed offers an excellent way to see nonverbal activities.

OBSERVING

Observing is being present or available to the messages that parishioners give through their bodies. These messages are communicated nonverbally through posture, facial expression, focus, movement, and reactions.

The importance of body messages is established by Mehrabian's research (Egan 1982b, 63–64) in the area of nonverbal behavior. He states a formula for how liking is expressed to another: "Total liking equals 7 percent verbal liking plus 38 percent vocal liking plus 55 percent facial liking." He then draws these implications: "Thus the impact of facial expression is the greatest, then the impact of the tone of voice (or vocal expression), and finally that of the words. If the facial expression is inconsistent with the words, the degree of liking conveyed by the facial expression will dominate and determine the impact of the total message."

Facial expression clearly has the greatest impact on the other person, but skilled pastors also need to be attentive to posture, focus of attention, movements, and reactions. Key facial expressions are: frowns, smiles, widening and narrowing of eyes, and lip and eyebrow movements. Posture clues include slouching, leaning forward or backward, military-like straightness, crossed legs. Focus means such things as looking at the pastor, facing the floor, focusing on some other person or object. Movements include: gestures (their speed and focus), pacing, changing head positions, and body shifts. Reactions are involuntary responses: breathing (both the speed and depth), blushing, crying, and sighing.

Body messages give important clues for understanding a parishioner's statements because the body conveys information about the person's feelings. Nonverbal data are especially valuable data because they are usually more spontaneous and less contrived than verbal responses. Thus, they can help us interpret a parishioner's statements by agreeing with, disagreeing with, or indicating the intensity of verbal responses. A person who is smiling while professing to be angry illustrates a nonverbal disagreement with the verbal message. An example of a nonverbal clue indicating the intensity of the message is a pronounced frown accompanying the statement "I am a little concerned."

Although a few nonverbal messages such as the smile and the frown have a universal meaning, body messages need to be interpreted in the context of sociological information, personal style, and conversational content in order to understand their specific meaning in a particular conversation. Sociological information includes: gender, age, race, class, subculture, and occupation. These factors should be combined with a knowledge of the particular style of the parishioner being observed because every individual is different. When the above examples are viewed again, the importance of these factors becomes even more apparent. In the first instance, smiling while being angry has become common in the United States. In the second instance, a particular parishioner might frown regularly due to a headache or some other problem and not the content of his or her statements.

Provisional interpretations of a parishioner's feelings concerning the content of the conversation, willingness to engage in the task of growth, and relationship with the pastor are important in pastoral conversations. Pastors make a tentative reading of these from observing the parishioner's postures, facial expressions, focuses of attention, movements, and reactions. For example, a slumped posture, down-turned mouth, face facing the floor, slow hand movements, and sighing would suggest a provisional interpretation that a parishioner was having some difficulty relating to the material, the task, the pastor, or some combination of these. This understanding is provisional because each of these nonverbal clues can have other meanings, depending on conversational content and personal and sociological factors. Thus, pastors continually need to test their interpretations during conversations and in later reflections.

An important standard for testing the importance and meaning of observed data is change during the conversation. For instance, if the person described in the previous paragraph sat up straight, looked the pastor in the eye, smiled, began to make more rapid gestures, and breathed in a more natural way, this would indicate that something important had happened. The pastor should try to reconstruct the context of the change. What was going on when it happened? Suppose this change occurred immediately after the pastor said, "I notice that you are facing the floor. I wonder if you feel somewhat uncomfortable talking with me?" Then the meaning of the nonverbal behaviors would likely be that the parishioner indeed has difficulty in the relationship with the pastor.

Observing, then, is an important skill because nonverbal clues play the major role in communicating feelings, and understanding feelings is the key to empathy. These body messages affect us whether or not we are aware of them; when we respond to them unconsciously, we respond on the basis of our personal and cultural prejudices. Because nonverbal messages do not have universal meanings they must be understood in terms of conversational content and the parishioner's sociological context and personal style. Thus, pastors practice being conscious of body messages so that they can reflect on their meaning for the parishioner rather than just react to the message in terms of their meaning for themselves. With skill in observing, pastors can make provisional interpretations about a parishioner's feelings about conversation content, the task of growth, and the relationship with the pastor.

LISTENING   *hear emotions*

Listening is being present to parishioners' words and manner of speaking. Spoken messages are a combination of the verbal content and the nonverbal delivery. Listening is the process of heeding and making provisional interpretations based on both types of audial data.

Delivery

The relative importance of the manner of speaking and the content is also established by Mehrabian's formula (Egan 1982b, 63–64): "Total liking equals 7 percent *verbal* liking plus 38 percent *vocal* liking plus 55 percent *facial* liking" (emphasis added). Thus the delivery is almost as important as the visual nonverbals and much more important than the words.

Many types of voice clues can be discerned from parishioners' manners of speaking. Egan (1982b, 64) lists tone of voice, pitch, voice level, intensity, inflection, spacing of words, emphases, pauses, silences, and fluency as important. Because of this abundance of types, Carkhuff (1979, 49) suggests that helpers simplify by focusing on two—voice level (softness or loudness) and rapidity of speech—and any changes in them.

Like the visual nonverbals, audial nonverbals help us understand parishioners' statements by conveying information about their feelings. Audial nonverbals also do this by agreeing with, disagreeing with, or indicating the intensity of verbal responses. For example, a woman who speaks very loudly (or very softly) while saying that she is angry displays agreement between her content and delivery. In contrast, a man who shouts at a child while saying that he is not upset with the child has some disagreement between nonverbal and verbal messages.

The manner of speaking, along with other nonverbals, signals the parts of parishioners' stories that are emotionally relevant to them. These emotionally charged items are the ones that are the most important for understanding parishioners' perspectives—the goal of stage 1. Voice clues, like visual nonverbals, need to be understood in the context of sociological information, personal style, and conversational content. For instance, a person's slow, deliberate speech may be a regional characteristic (sociological), a habit (personal style), or a clue that the subject matter is difficult to talk about (content).

Content

Listening involves grasping the content of parishioners' statements—understanding what they mean by the words they use and the way they organize those words. Thus it includes noticing what is not said as well as noticing what is said specifically and what is said as a generalization.

The content of parishioners' statements can be organized into four categories—feelings, experiences, actions, and thoughts—and can be remembered by the acronym FEAT.

F　*Feelings* are the emotions that parishioners have about their experiences, actions, and thoughts. Feelings are internal experiences. If a student states, "I feel awful about the course," she is focusing on her emotions about the course. Though feelings are a response to the other three categories, I have listed them first as a reminder that they are the primary category to listen for. As I have said before, understanding feelings is the key to empathy.

E　*Experiences* are things that parishioners perceive as *happening to* them. If a student states, "Professor Smith flunked me," she is discussing her problem as an experience. Experiences can be external or internal. For instance, being hit by a car is an external experience, whereas being overcome with fear is an internal one. The distinguishing aspect of any experience is that it is understood as *happening to* persons. Many parishioners tell their stories primarily in terms of experiences because they see themselves as victims of forces beyond their control.

A   *Actions* are what parishioners *do or do not do*. If the student we have been discussing states, "I did not pass the course because I didn't study enough," she would be talking about it as an action. When parishioners discuss their actions they are taking some responsibility in the situation.

T   *Thoughts* are internal activities or behaviors that parishioners *do or do not do*. This category includes: fantasies, daydreams, meditations, attitudes, decisions, prayers, memories, plans, ideas, values, beliefs, and similar covert actions. For instance, if the student in the illustration said, "I feel that it's unfair that I failed," she would be discussing a thought. Because thoughts are behaviors they are learned and can be unlearned.

FEAT.   The FEAT categories are important in helping pastors notice what is said and not said. FEAT categories inspire questions such as: Is the parishioner discussing both the experience and her or his actions and thoughts? Is the parishioner expressing his or her feelings about the experience, actions, and thoughts? Has the parishioner expressed her or his specific experiences, actions, and thoughts? Of particular importance is the question, What are the thoughts (beliefs, rules, statements) that lie behind the parishioner's feelings or actions?

It is as necessary to understand words in context as it is to so understand nonverbals. The meaning of words is almost as dependent on sociological information, personal style, and conversational content as nonverbals are. For instance, the word *bad* means evil or poor among members of white middle-class culture, whereas it often means very good in African-American slang (this second meaning now has a wider cultural use). Personal style also determines the meaning of a word; one person may consistently use the word *angry* to mean a tiny bit perturbed, while another person may reserve it for describing actively acted-out rage. The context of a conversation often indicates the meaning of a word. In the statement "I love all the people in the world," the phrase "all the people in the world" puts the word *love* in a different context from its context in the statement "I love my wife more than any person or thing in the world." The word *love* probably has a different meaning in these two statements.

In sum, listening is the skill of perceiving what parishioners mean by the words they use and the way they speak them. The delivery of the words provides the primary clues for understanding parishioners' meanings; nonverbals such as voice level and rapidity of speech are especially helpful in highlighting the emotionally relevant statements. One way of making sense of the messages is to categorize them as feelings, experiences, actions, and thoughts. Both the nonverbal and the verbal messages must be understood in the context of sociological information, personal style, and conversational content.

PROBLEMS IN ATTENDING

Three major factors cause problems in attending: distractions, evaluations, and differences, and can be remembered by the acronym DED.

D   *Distractions* are needs or issues of pastors that interfere with their attentiveness to parishioners. Some common distractions can be grouped in the following manner.

- Physical condition. We are too tired or sick to do the hard work of observing and listening. Often we are either not aware of our tiredness or we think, wrongly, that we can be effective in spite of our physical condition.
- Anxiety. We are so eager to respond, solve the problem, impress parishioners, or get to the next responsibility that we only listen to part of parishioners' statements.
- Guilt. We are so concerned about the things we have done or left undone that we have difficulty focusing on parishioners. The content of parishioners' stories may touch some area, like sex or divorce, that we are guilty about.
- Anger-Love. We become so intent on our feelings of attraction toward or alienation from parishioners that we cannot fully attend to them.

It is impossible to avoid having these feelings. It is important, however, to be aware of these distractions and the way they affect pastors. Pastors need to look for distractions within themselves, acknowledge them, let them go, and attend to the parishioner with renewed focus. With this acceptance and awareness pastors are better able to attend.

E   *Evaluations* are judgments of parishioners' statements in terms of good and bad, right and wrong, deserving of sympathy and deserving of reproach. Both negative judgments, which engage us in disputing parishioners' statements, and positive judgments, which involve us in agreeing with them, interfere with our ability to understand their points of view—the pastoral task in stage 1. Pastors are called to practice listening nonjudgmentally, simply accepting parishioners' statements as their descriptions of their experience. When pastors realize that they are evaluating, it is important that they acknowledge the evaluations, recognize them as their own issues about themselves and not the parishioners, and try to let them go.

D *Differences* describe the sociological and personal filters that are part of all observing and listening, barriers that make it difficult to understand others and their points of view. On the positive side, these filters are important for our mental health because they keep us from having to pay attention to everything in the continuous and overwhelming stream of data that attacks our consciousness. On the negative side, these filters make it difficult to understand the messages of those who pay attention to different data in the stream.

The story about the ambassador's dandruff (Condon & Yousef 1975, 1) shows the effect of a sociological filter. In a conversation about a former U.S. ambassador, between the authors and some Japanese students in Tokyo, one woman remarked, "Yes, he was excellent, but I think his wife was not such a good wife, if you know what I mean." The authors did not know what she meant; nor were they illumined by the clarification that she had seen him on television several times and "noticed that he had dandruff on his shoulders." Yet the other students understood this explanation. They explained to Condon and Yousef that in Japan a good wife is responsible for her husband's personal appearance: therefore, the ambassador's poor grooming was obviously his wife's fault. Because of this sociological filter, the fact of the dandruff was so striking to the woman that she remembered it but did not recall anything that the ambassador had said.

A personal filter is one that is related to a person's makeup. For instance, Walter Chang is intensely interested in music. Although he is a clerk in a shoe store, he thinks of people primarily in terms of their musical tastes. This is a personal filter because his interest in music is not a characteristic related to his belonging to such sociological groups as Asian-Americans, males, lower middle class, and shoe store clerks.

Pastors can develop their ability to empathize in spite of differences by doing two things: first, admitting that they do not understand; and second, taking the other person's point of view seriously by asking for help in understanding them. Although pastors can never attend perfectly because of their sociological groupings, personal filters, ingrained evaluations, and unresolved guilt, anxiety, and anger or love, it is important for pastors to work on problems in attending by working through their own issues by means of prayer, counseling, and supervision. If a pastor is unable to deal with the distractions, evaluations, or differences in caring for a particular parishioner, it is important to either refer the person to another pastor or work through the problem with a supervisor.

LEARNING THE SKILLS

The attending skills of positioning, observing, and listening are the most important of the helping skills because all the others depend on them. It is through orienting ourselves physically, taking note of visual nonverbals, and paying attention to the manner of speaking and the words spoken that we gain the data from which to develop an understanding of another's point of view. Without this information there can be no helping.

The nonverbal cues that we see and hear and the words that we hear are not self-explanatory. They must be interpreted in the context of sociological information, personal style, and conversational content to reveal their full meaning. A key way of identifying important nonverbal data is by noting changes during the conversation. The context determines the meaning of the nonverbal data.

Nonverbals are more important to notice than words because they are more likely to reveal true feelings. Thus, the pastor can interpret parishioners' words by noting whether the nonverbals agree, disagree, or add intensity.

Distractions, evaluations, and differences (DED) are three factors that cause problems in attending. Tiredness or illness, anxiousness, guilt, anger, or love will distract us, interfering with our attending. Likewise, negative or positive evaluations will also get in the way. But most of all, differences such as gender, age, race, and subculture create barriers to attending. Attending skills are very much affected by pastors' emotional and spiritual states.

Finally, even though pastors work hard at resolving distractions, suspending judgments, and understanding differences, pastors will misperceive some parishioners' communications. That is why the responding skills are so important—they offer parishioners a comfortable chance to correct pastors' misperceptions.

Process

Reading about skills is not enough. In order to learn to use them effectively we must understand the concepts by reading and discussion. Then we learn to discriminate between correct and incorrect use of skills by exercises or by watching others, and follow up by practicing communicating feedback to them. The process of learning the helping skills is much like that of learning a language—one has to practice and practice until the new way of communicating becomes natural. That is why I call learning the pastoral skills "learning the language of care."

Because the most effective way to learn to discriminate and communicate the skills is through *practice groups,* I will discuss them here in detail. Practice groups consist of three or more people who meet to practice the skills. One person plays the role of parishioner, another the pastor, and the rest are observers. There should be a moderator of the session; either an instructor or an observer can take this role.

The practice can be done using either role-play issues or the participants' own issues. In a role play the participants act out a situation other than their own but supply dialogue, emotions, and gestures from their own imaginations and experiences. The advantage of role play is that participants have less trouble shifting from considering the problem to reflecting on skills when the problems are not their own. On the other hand, practicing with real issues gives participating pastors the experience of dealing with parishioners' spontaneous responses, and it also gives participating parishioners the experience and help that come from actually receiving pastoral care. I prefer the practice with real issues because I think that the spontaneity of response and the empathy developed by being a real parishioner outweigh the difficulties in keeping the focus on the skills.

Roles. The pastor's duties are to establish goals for the session, converse with the parishioner, and participate in the feedback session. The parishioner's duties are to present an issue for the conversation, participate genuinely in the conversation, and give feedback to the pastor during the feedback discussion. The observers' duties are to note the nonverbals of the pastor and parishioner and the content and feelings expressed in the verbal exchanges, and to give feedback to the pastor about her or his strengths and weaknesses in using the skill(s). The moderator's duties are to ascertain the pastor's goals before the conversation, assign specific duties to the observers, keep time, supervise the taping (if applicable), and lead the feedback session.

Debriefing.   The order of debriefing is parishioner first, then pastor, and then the observer(s). The moderator inquires first about how the parishioner is feeling in order to identify and handle any feelings or issues that are left over from being counseled. After these are dealt with, the moderator asks the parishioner to comment on the helpful and unhelpful things the pastor did. Next the pastor is asked about her or his feelings, after which she or he is invited to ask for specific feedback from the parishioner and the observer(s). After responding to the pastor's questions, the observers (moderator last) give feedback on the areas they were assigned to monitor. When necessary two persons can practice with a video or audiotape as the observer. In these situations the pastor would take the moderator's role with the following modifications: After inquiring about and processing the parishioner's feelings, the parishioner would do the same for the pastor. Then they would play the tape and discuss it.

Exercises

1. Positioning

    A. Finding Your Own Version of SOLER. Try sitting in the SOLER position, adjusting it until you feel fairly comfortable. Practice using this position in conversations. Making allowances for the normal physical discomfort and self-consciousness of trying a new position, note any differences that this position makes in yourself and in others' response to you. Write down your observations.

    B. Noticing the Effect of Positioning in a Group. Sit in a circle with a group and discuss some topic of mutual interest for three to five minutes. Have several participants adopt non-SOLER positions while participating in the discussion. After the discussion, share your reactions to both those in the SOLER position and those in the non-SOLER positions.

    C. Observing Positioning. Observe three conversations (live, TV, or movie) outside the practice group. Write down your observations and interpretations in response to these questions: (1) How did the participants' positioning indicate interest? (2) How did the participants' positioning affect the other participant(s)? (3) How did such sociological factors as gender, social roles, relationships, race, or subculture affect the participants' positioning?

2. *Observing* (this exercise should be repeated until you are competent and comfortable with this skill).

Draw a chart like that in the example below. Observe a conversation for five minutes making notes on the chart about the parishioner's initial appearance, any subsequent changes, and the context of the change. Last, categorize the nonverbals by whether they agreed with, disagreed with, or added intensity to the verbal statements.

For example, let us make a chart for the following exchange. A pastor says to a parishioner, "I notice that you are facing the floor. I wonder if you feel somewhat uncomfortable talking with me?" The parishioner replies, "A little bit."

Nonverbals	*Initial*	*Change*	*Context (mention of)*
Posture:	slumped	sat up	posture
Expression:	down-turned mouth	smile	expression
Focus:	facing floor	eye contact	focus
Movements:	slow hand motions	rapid gestures	movements
Reactions:	shallow breathing	deeper breathing	reactions

INTERPRETATION: These nonverbals added intensity to the parishioner's response.

3. *Listening* (these exercises should be repeated until you are competent and comfortable with these skills).

A. Noting Voice Level and Rapidity. Listen to a conversation (live, TV, or tape) for five minutes. Note the changes in voice level and rapidity on a chart (see example below). Interpret these changes by determining what information it gave (agreed with, disagreed with, or added emphasis to the person's statement) and what was the reason for this change (context, personal style, or sociological grouping). If this exercise is done with other observers, have a discussion about your various interpretations.

Example

Statement	*Change*	*Information*	*Reason*
I am very angry	voice quieter	emphasis	sociological

B. Categorizing Statements in Terms of Feelings, Experiences, Actions, and Thoughts. Listen to a pastoral conversation for five minutes, taking notes on key statements about the parishioner's problem or joy. Analyze each statement by categorizing its dominant theme as either feelings, experiences, actions, or thoughts. Then note any secondary theme. If this exercise is done with others, discuss your categorizations of the various statements.

For example, analyze the following statements: This has been the worst week of my life—everything is happening to me. First, my kid gets put out of school; then my boss gives me trouble; and finally my husband starts acting up about nothing. It's just awful.

Interpretation: The dominant theme is experiences, "Everything is happening to me." The secondary theme is feelings, ". . . worst week. . . . It's just awful."

Handwritten margin notes:
① Help me to understand
② seems as like of statement
③ say a portion question form
④ "Because"
⑤ "Tell me"
① to clarify what you heard
② get them to go deeper

2
Responding

TWO RESPONDING SKILLS are key: paraphrasing and probing. *Paraphrasing* is restating (in the pastor's words) the central feelings and content of a parishioner's statements. *Probing* is asking for clarification.

Pastors use these central responding skills to aid parishioners in exploring their issues. Paraphrases and probes let parishioners rehear what they are saying, as well as telling them how they are being understood—two helps to their exploration. Responding skills are important for pastors because these skills help them understand parishioners' feelings, experiences, actions, and thoughts. Thus, pastors use responding skills both to gain and express empathy.

CONCERNS ABOUT
CHANGES IN WORSHIP

Two conversations (adapted from Jacobs 1985, 3–5) can illustrate the difference that the responding skills can make in a pastoral conversation. The concern over the language used in worship is common to a number of traditions that struggle between Elizabethan forms and more modern expressions. In this instance, Robert, the pastor of St. Jerome's, has led his congregation in adopting the new Book of Common Prayer (1979). He is in his office between worship services. A parishioner, Anne, has come to the door without an appointment. She still favors the language used in the 1928 edition of the prayer book. Both know that the time for conversation will be brief.

Robert Counters Anne

ANNE: I've come to see you because I'm very unhappy about our using the new prayer book. I'm thinking of changing churches and going to St. Swithin's.

ROBERT: Well, the bishop has said that we are to use the new prayer book. The church must keep up with the times.

ANNE: I can't change just like that—I've been a member here for twenty years. I think that a lot of dignity has gone out of the service.

ROBERT: [*Speaking louder and more rapidly*] What do you mean, dignity's gone out of the service? That's not true at all. I was trained to do things well, and I've continued to do that in the new service.

ANNE: I don't mean to hurt your feelings. I . . . well . . . I feel that all those "yous" and "yours" and the elimination of some of my favorite prayers are no improvement on the 1928 Book of Common Prayer. Obviously, if I feel that way, I'm not in line with others here, and I ought to go somewhere where I fit in.

ROBERT: But you've always been here—you can't leave just like that. I appreciate all you've done for us—you've always been so generous in the support of this church.

ANNE: It doesn't make any difference. We're all part of the same church after all. I'd sooner give my money to a parish that upholds the old standards, like St. Swithin's.

ROBERT: But St. Swithin's might change too . . . where would you be then? Anyway, St. Swithin's is not your type of church at all; it is too ceremonial for you.

ANNE: It's how this place used to be before all the changes. I blame the last pastor, actually, he was the one that started it; and then he ran off with the director of religious education . . . well I mean, there's standards for you. I don't blame you, you haven't been here long.

ROBERT: I don't think we should criticize Father John. He's not here to answer for himself. I can't change things back again. Everyone else is happy with the new setup.

ANNE: That's what I mean . . . I think it's best if I go. . . .

Robert Responds to Anne

ANNE: I dropped by because I'm very unhappy about our using the new prayer book. I'm thinking of changing churches and going to St. Swithin's.

ROBERT: St. Swithin's?

ANNE: Yes, they do things differently there. They haven't changed their prayer book.

ROBERT: And you think St. Swithin's would suit you.

ANNE: Yes . . . well, it's not an easy decision. I've been a member of this church for twenty years and I won't find it easy to move. St. Swithin's is a bit too ceremonial for me. But at least they haven't got all those "yous" and "yours" and plain-language prayers. None of that's an improvement on the 1928 Book of Common Prayer.

ROBERT: You feel so bad because we are using the new prayer book that you're considering leaving here after twenty years and going somewhere that doesn't really have your type of ritual.

ANNE: It *is* a difficult decision. But I feel I'm the one who's out of step. Everyone else seems happy with the changes.

ROBERT: I'm not sure that's true. There *are* others who feel the way you do—you must know them—I guess you discuss it among yourselves at times.

ANNE: One or two. And I don't particularly want to lose contact with them. We've grown up here together.

ROBERT: And they don't want to leave us?

ANNE: No—but perhaps they don't worry about dignity like I do.

ROBERT: [*Encouragingly*] Dignity? Do you mean your dignity, or the service?

ANNE: The service, of course.

ROBERT: You feel the service lacks dignity.

ANNE: Yes. It's probably very good for the young people and the families with children. It's not your fault; the church has to look after the young. I blame the last pastor actually, he started it all, introducing the changes.

ROBERT: There were a number of things that were difficult then, weren't there? But I've introduced some changes too . . . perhaps you're feeling that the church here has lost some dignity, and that the clergy are to blame.

ANNE: I suppose so. [*Pause*] I don't know.

ROBERT: Well, I wonder what we can do to improve things for you and those who feel like you. Would it be a good idea to consider that first rather than lose you? It sounds as if you've got your values too, and that we should talk about those.

ANNE: Yes, I had hoped you would say that . . .

Analysis

In the first conversation, Robert's responses are not directed toward helping Anne, the parishioner, explore the problem. Robert's first response is an informational defense. His second is a disagreement with Anne's statement. Then the pastor argues by self-sharing in the third response, and disagrees with the parishioner's statement again in the fourth. Robert's fifth statement is defensive. This pastor does not use the responding skills of paraphrasing and probing, and the result is that empathy is not expressed. Instead, the pastor is in a defensive role. From that posture Robert misunderstands Anne's feeling of ambivalence—wanting both to stay and to go—expressed in her first two statements. The pastor disrespects the parishioner—by judging her third and fourth statements. Finally, Robert does not promote clarity about the parishioner's feelings, experiences, actions, and thoughts.

In sum, because the pastoral relationship is not established by using the responding skills, the conflict moves toward dissolution rather than resolution.

In the second conversation, Robert helps Anne explore the problem by using the presence skills. The first response is a probe; the second and third are paraphrases. Next, the pastor uses a proclamation skill—information giving. Robert then uses responding skills to examine Anne's response to that information. Thus, the pastor's fifth and sixth responses are probes and the seventh is a paraphrase. The eighth is a hunch, an assessment skill, attempting to get at the deep feeling underlying Anne's concerns. Since she was unwilling to share that feeling directly, and time was pressing, Robert moved quickly to a stage 3 invitation to action. Because the pastoral relationship was established by the use of the responding skills, pastor and parishioner could quickly consider moving to collaborative problem solving.

PARAPHRASING

Paraphrasing is restating, in one's own words, the core of parishioners' statements. Restatement is important because it either shows that pastors understand, alleviating parishioners' painful sense of being alone and not understood, or it exposes *inevitable* misunderstandings, giving parishioners easy opportunities to correct them. Either way, paraphrasing helps parishioners hear the core of their statements; this second hearing enables them to understand their stories better. Paraphrasing is a more important skill than any of the other responses discussed throughout this book because it is the one that contributes most to both parishioners' exploring and pastors' empathy.

Carkhuff (1983a) has developed a formula for paraphrasing feeling and content: You feel _____ because _____. This formula puts feeling in its primary place and makes the content (experiences, actions, and thoughts) an explanation for the feeling. The core of some statements is only feeling, others only content; the paraphrases of such statements should include just feeling or content. The formula for feeling alone is,

②You feel _____. The formula for content alone is, You are saying
_____. If the core of parishioners' statements has both feelings
and content, then the paraphrases should include both unless you choose
to focus on one or the other. Although there are many other ways to
formulate a paraphrase, Carkhuff's formulas are important to remember as
standards for designing and evaluating paraphrases.

To illustrate different paraphrases, imagine hearing the following complaint by a choir member, who speaks slowly, crisply, with a tight face,
and a rigid body posture: "Everything is going downhill in the choir, nothing
is getting done; no music is being rehearsed; the practices are unruly; it's
not right that I should have to participate in an organization like that."

1. Paraphrase of feeling and content: "You feel irritated because things
   are not going well in the choir."
2. Content paraphrase: "You are saying that the way things are going
   makes it difficult for you to participate in the choir."
3. Feeling paraphrase: "You are feeling upset."

Guidelines for Paraphrasing

Four guidelines for good paraphrases need to be remembered: paraphrasing
is not parroting, paraphrases suspend judgment, paraphrases do not include
hunches, and paraphrases are brief. These guidelines are illustrated by
responses to the choir member's complaint.

Do not parrot.   Parroting is echoing or repeating parishioners' statements, whereas paraphrasing is putting their feelings and content into one's
own words. Putting statements into one's own words does two things: first,
it helps the pastor increase his or her understanding of others' statements;
and second, it highlights our misunderstandings. An example of parroting
the choir member's statement is: "You are saying that everything is going
downhill in the choir."

Suspend judgment.   Paraphrases restate parishioners' statements but do
not judge them. This means that pastors are to reflect back perceptions,
whether or not one agrees with them, without indicating one's agreement
or disagreement. Two examples in which judgment has not been suspended
are: "You feel upset because you think things are awful in the choir, but
I wonder if they are as bad as you say?" or "I certainly understand your
being upset with the way things are going in *that* choir."

Forgo hunches. Paraphrases are interchangeable with parishioners' statements and should not include guesses about implied feelings and contents. An example of a poor paraphrase that contains a hunch is: "You are upset with what is going on in the choir because you don't like the new choir director."

Be brief. Long responses distract parishioners, causing them to turn from understanding their own story to trying to understand our paraphrases. An example of an accurate but overly long paraphrase is: "You are saying that there are just a lot of things going wrong in the choir—all kinds of things. First, it does not seem that the choir is doing its job. Second, the quality of the music rehearsal is poor. Third, the practices are out of control. There is not the kind of discipline that would be helpful in this type of situation. Therefore you are upset with having to be in such a situation."

PARAPHRASING FEELINGS

Feelings are important indicators of what people value and what is giving them difficulty. When these feelings are not acknowledged by pastors, the solutions parishioners develop will be neither relevant nor carried out. Gaylin (1979, 3) sums up the function of feelings in this way: "Feelings are the fine instruments which shape decision making in an animal cursed and blessed with intelligence, and the freedom which is its corollary. They are signals directing us toward goodness, safety, pleasure, and group survival." Thus, pastors need to consider parishioners' feelings before encouraging them to move toward problem solving because parishioners need to become aware of their "fine instruments."

Feelings also locate what it is about a situation that causes difficulty for the person. Again, although the situation is never the whole problem, the person's perspective contributes to his or her difficulty in handling the problem. In the example of the choir member's complaint, part of the difficulty is the angry feelings about the situation in the choir. These feelings make it difficult for the choir member either to enjoy or work toward changing the situation. In this example the belief behind the feelings is explicit: "It's not right that I have to participate in an organization like that." Often the underlying beliefs that block resolution of the problem are not explicitly stated; they need to be uncovered by exploring the feelings.

Even though feelings are basic to understanding the problem, pastors often neglect to include them in their paraphrases. First, feelings are hard to identify. Gaylin (1979, 10) describes them as "difficult to quantify, difficult to communicate, difficult even to distinguish within ourselves one from another." Added to these obstacles are differences caused by personal style, sociological grouping, and conversational context. To further complicate identification, people often consciously try to hide their emotions from others. A greater impediment is *repression*—the feelings have been pushed out of awareness; they are hidden by parishioners from themselves.

Second, facing feelings is often distressing. Angry, guilty, and anxious feelings are painful for both parishioners and pastors. The purpose of the distress is to spur action on the problem, but people often try to get rid of the distress instead of acting on the problem. For instance, we try to get rid of guilty feelings by arguing them away or by employing self-distractions such as work, drink, drugs, sex, or eating. The correct resolution of the distress is to explore the feelings, understand both the underlying beliefs that cause them and the gospel response to those beliefs, and take appropriate action.

Negative Feelings and the Pastoral Role

The pastoral role raises special problems in responding to feelings. For instance, some parishioners try to hide feelings from pastors because they are reluctant to express bad feelings such as anger, guilt, or anxiety to a representative of God and the church. In addition, parishioners sometimes use their religion as an escape from their negative feelings; they pray hard to get rid of their feelings instead of changing the beliefs that cause them. Often parishioners use their active involvement in church or community programs to avoid dealing with their feelings. They literally engage in furious service.

Paraphrases are brief, respectful, and interchangeable statements, in pastors' own words, of parishioners' core messages. The most complete paraphrases include both feeling and content, but some restate either feeling or content only. Although feelings are difficult to identify and sometimes painful to deal with, they are the key to both understanding parishioners and successful problem solving. Therefore, pastors need to help parishioners express feelings through paraphrasing. Through the process of expressing feelings to God and the pastor, parishioners experience the good news of God's in-spite-of acceptance.

 **PROBING**

Probing is asking for clarification. Probes help parishioners speak more concretely about their feelings, experiences, actions, and thoughts. They help pastors, also, to get the information needed to understand parishioners' perspectives.

Four Types of Probes

Egan (1982, 100–04) lists four common types of probes: minimal prompts, accents, statements, and questions.

Minimal prompts.   Minimal prompts are brief verbal activities such as "uh-huh," "hmmm," "yes," "I see," "ah," and "oh." The least amount of pastors' agendas is conveyed in this type. Thus, parishioners' responses to them are usually the most revealing of their own agendas. For example, a parishioner says, "It feels funny when I think about the fact that I am going to start college in just three weeks." One minimal prompt would be, "Hmmm."

Accents.   Accents are repetitions of one, two, or three words of parishioners' statements. Accents guide parishioners' responses more than minimal prompts do, yet they are much more open-ended than statements or questions. For example, the same statement is given: "It feels funny when I think about the fact that I am going to start college in just three weeks." One accent would be, "Funny?"

Statements.   Statements are in the indicative form, yet when they are given in a tentative tone of voice they invite the parishioner to be more specific. They are more open-ended and less intrusive than questions but not as gentle as minimal prompts and accents. For example, to the same statement: "It feels funny when I think about the fact that I am going to start college in just three weeks," the pastor may respond with a statement like: "I imagine going to college is both exciting and scary."

Questions.   Questions are a sentence in an interrogative form. In ordinary conversations, they are the most common form of probe. Because questions are experienced as more intrusive than accents, minimal prompts, and statements, skilled pastors do not use them as often as these other probes. The example is, again, the parishioner's statement, "It feels funny when I think about the fact that I am going to start college in just three weeks." The pastor may pose a question in reply: "What do you mean by funny?"

Guidelines for Probing

Unskilled pastors tend to use too many and unhelpful probes. This occurs when pastors lose track of the goal of the responding skills—helping the parishioner to explore. Instead, pastors can get involved in trying to understand all of the details of the story for their own purposes. The following five guidelines give clear directions for the use of probes.

Focus on concrete expressions. Probes can be used to help parishioners express themselves more concretely. Parishioners are helped by talking more specifically about their feelings and their reasons (experiences, actions, and thoughts) for these feelings. This helps them to become more aware of their own perspectives and the role they play in the situation.

If a parishioner says, "I have been trying all day to figure out which dress I should wear tonight," an example of this kind of probe is for the pastor to answer, "Tell me a little more about why it's so difficult to decide."

Seek the parishioners' perspectives. Probes can be used to help pastors understand parishioners' perspectives. Because skilled pastors have the stage 1 goal of understanding parishioners' perspectives, they focus on understanding their feelings and the reasons for them. In contrast, unskilled pastors think that their role is to solve the problem for the parishioners; thus, they focus on getting comprehensive information about the problem.

For example, a parishioner may confide in a pastor by saying, "I am not sure who it is I am supposed to be helping—the employees who are having a hard time and need help, the investors who deserve a fair return, or the consumer who should get a quality product at the lowest price." A probe for perspective by the pastor is: "How does that make you feel?" By contrast, a probe for information is: "What are the merits of the employees', investors', and consumers' claims on you as a Christian?"

Make probes open-ended. Open-ended probes encourage parishioners to examine their FEAT, leading them to a greater understanding of their problems or joys. Closed questions force parishioners to think in terms of pastors' agendas. If a parishioner states, "I really look forward to getting married," the accent "Look forward?" is an open-ended response. The question "Is it the wedding or the honeymoon that you are excited about?" is an example of a closed response.

Avoid interrogation. Probes should not be asked in succession. There should be paraphrases between questions to help parishioners explore their answers and to keep them from feeling that they are being interrogated. For example, a parishioner may say to the pastor, "I expect you to teach my son all about the Bible in your Sunday school class." The pastor replies, "I'm not sure what you mean." The parishioner elaborates, "You know . . . teach him that it is the Word of God and that he has to respect it and everything." The pastor then paraphrases, saying, for example, "You are concerned because you want him to gain a reverence for the Scriptures." The parishioner replies, "Yes, I am worried about Johnny because he doesn't seem to be interested in reading the Bible since he started studying evolution and all that stuff."

Allow silence.   Probes should not be asked just to fill the silence. Silences are important parts of conversations because parishioners and pastors do the necessary work of reflection during them. After a period of silence it is often helpful to ask the parishioner what went on in the silence.

Probing is an important skill because it can help both pastors and parishioners to a more concrete understanding of parishioners' perspectives. The most helpful probes are less intrusive and more open-ended, such as accents and minimal prompts. Probes can be misused by focusing on information instead of perspective, using them one right after another, and probing to fill the silence. Though probing is a basic responding skill, skilled pastors will normally use twice as many paraphrases as probes to ensure that they are focusing on helping parishioners to explore their own stories rather than the pastors' agendas.

LEARNING THE SKILLS

The responding skills are verbal ways of communicating our presence. Paraphrasing lets parishioners know that we are listening—they are not alone because someone understands. Probing shows our concern to understand their stories. The responding skills are the primary way of expressing empathy—our understanding of their perspective.

Unskilled pastors characteristically make two major mistakes in using the responding skills. First, they paraphrase content but not feeling; thus, they miss the key to understanding parishioners' perspectives. Second, they use too many probes; this has the effect of shifting the conversation from parishioners' exploring to pastors' agendas.

The responding skills are designed to keep us focused on parishioners themselves—their feelings, experiences, actions, and thoughts—instead of on our interests or their problems. This focus on parishioners communicates our care and establishes the type of relationship that helps them to explore, understand, and act.

Process

The process of learning the language of care is much like the process of learning any language. One has to practice and practice until the new way of communicating becomes natural.

When people begin to learn the pastoral skills they feel unnatural and clumsy. People often feel more incompetent after they begin skills training than before. This is to be expected because they were unconscious of their limited competence when they began. Once they started to learn they became conscious of their limited competence—thus the feeling of incompetence. It takes a great deal of practice to move to the third phase—conscious competence. Though pastors are much more helpful to parishioners in this phase than they were before skill training, this third phase is still not as comfortable as being unconscious. Finally, after much more practice pastors can reach the fourth phase, unconscious competence. This last phase is both comfortable for the pastor and helpful for the parishioner.

An inspiring image for this process is the journey of the Israelites from Egypt to the promised land. They escaped the bondage of Egypt (unconsciously less competent) and crossed over the Red Sea into the wilderness (consciously less competent). They soon wished they were back in Egypt because freedom caused discomfort; they missed their old securities. After a time in the desert they became a people moving toward the promised land (consciously more competent). They spent less time complaining and more time organizing. Finally, after forty years, they were allowed to cross the Jordan into the promised land (unconsciously more competent). Like the journey of the Israelites, the process of learning pastoral skills is a movement from old bondages to new freedoms through a wilderness full of trials.

Exercises

1. *Practicing Paraphrasing*
    A. Paraphrase the central feeling and content themes of the following statements.
        i. I just don't have any reason to go to church now that they have messed it up with new prayer books, man-hating women pastors, and communist politics. It's just awful—it's not my church anymore. I used to love church so much. I used to work on the altar guild every week helping Pastor Smith. He certainly loved God—it was great working for him.

ii. I just don't understand why we have to pray out of the same book . . . say the same prayers all the time. Even the Roman Catholics don't do that anymore. My friend John showed me the little books they get each month, and the prayers are different all the time. I think that's what's wrong with us—no spirit. I don't mean to sound like I dislike our denomination, I am just concerned.

iii. I know that I shouldn't feel this way, but I get so angry at my children during worship. They just fidget, and talk, and bother each other. Then I have to stop praying and start getting them to act right. It just ruins worship for me. (*Pause*) I probably need to stay home. (*Pause*) I don't know what I should do. I am not sure why I feel this way. I didn't think I would be this kind of parent.

iv. I leave all of that theology stuff to you preachers. I just try to do my best. I try to treat people like they ought to be treated, and help out when and where I can. I am no saint, but I do my part. I have helped several people at the office, and I belong to several groups that help in the community, and I used to serve on the vestry.

Check the paraphrases to see if they include feelings and content (if the statement includes both), paraphrase instead of parrot, suspend judgment, exclude hunches, and are brief.

B. Practicing critiquing your paraphrases. Listen to a five-minute tape of one of your pastoral conversations. Then critique your paraphrases on the basis of their frequency, inclusion of feeling and content, use of your own words, lack of hunches, suspension of judgment, and brevity. Conclude by making a note of any unhelpful patterns that you discern.

C. Developing alternative leads for paraphrasing. Read the following list and memorize at least three alternative introductions. Then add any of your own that are not on the list.

Kind of feeling. . . , sort of saying. . . , As I get it, you felt. . . , If I'm hearing you correctly. . . , As I get it, you're saying. . . , Kind of made (makes) you feel. . . , I'm not sure I'm with you, but. . . , I really hear you saying that. . . , It sounds as if you're saying. . . , It appears to you. . . , It seems to you. . . , I gather. . . , (adapted from Hammond, Hepworth, and Smith, 1977, 114–15).

2. *Expanding Your Feeling Word Vocabulary*

Read over the list (adapted from Carkhuff 1983a, 255–58; Hammond, Hepworth, and Smith 1977, 86–87) and rank each word as strong (A), moderate (B), or weak (C) by putting an A, B, or C beside the word. Then add at least two words to each category. Conclude by discussing your results with others.

The feeling words are organized into six basic categories that form three pairs of opposites: Guilt and Acceptance, Anxiety and Hope, Anger and Love. The rationale for these categories is discussed in chapter 5.

GUILT. At fault, blew it, responsible, to blame, wrong.
  Shame. Ashamed, demeaned, disgraced, humiliated, redfaced. *Inadequacy.* Deficient, incompetent, unfit. *Embarrassment.* Awkward, dumb, foolish, self-conscious, silly. *Despair.* Insignificant, no good, stupid, unforgivable, worthless.
ACCEPTANCE. Admired, cherished, prized, revered.
  Forgiven. Comforted, freed, grateful, relieved, thankful, unburdened. *Confident.* Accepted, at ease, competent, sure, strong.

ANXIETY. Agitated, edgy, nervous, tense, uptight, worried.
  Frightened. Afraid, apprehensive, fearful, scared, threatened. *Confused.* Baffled, blank, foggy, lost, uncertain. *Dread.* Demoralized, hopeless, intimidated, overwhelmed, stressed, tired.
HOPE. Alive, eager, energized, excited, stimulated.
  Calm. Composed, mellow, peaceful, relaxed. *Competent.* Able, capable, in charge, powerful, qualified.

ANGER. Annoyed, displeased, frustrated, indignant, worked up.
  Distress. Afflicted, bothered, offended, troubled, upset. *Sad.* Awful, devastated, down, low, sorrowful, unhappy. *Alienation.* Bitter, bored, hostile, hurt, resentful, tired of.
LOVE. Attracted, close, enamored, fond of, like, warm.
  Caring. Admiration, concern, regard, tenderness toward. *Happy.* Cheerful, joyful, spirited, wonderful.

3. *Combining Paraphrasing and Probing*

Introducing probes with paraphrases is an important technique for two reasons. First, it makes the probe feel a lot less harsh to the parishioner. Second, it forces the pastor to relate the probe to the paraphrase—and therefore to the parishioner's statement. For example: A thirty-five-year-old former serviceman says to the pastor, "I have been thinking about reenlisting in the Army Reserve, but I am not sure whether or not I can do that and hold onto my Christian principles. I am really confused; I don't know what I should do." The pastor says, "You feel mixed-up because of the tension between the service and your beliefs and you don't know whether to reenlist or not. What ideas have come to you so far?"

A. For each of the following statements, paraphrase the central feeling and content themes, then add a probe.

    i. A nineteen-year-old female college student: "I have been thinking that I ought to get arrested in an antipollution demonstration. I mean, if the pollution isn't stopped, it's no use going to college anyway. My parents want me to ignore the world and keep my nose in the books. They think that they have the right to, like, run my life . . . just because they pay a few fees. I think being true to myself is more important. What do you think?"

    ii. A twenty-four-year-old man in his second year of marriage: "It's just not the same between us as it used to be. When we got married everything was so nice, now it's nothing but a hassle. I just want to get away from her. I know it's not what I promised in the service and all that, but there's got to be more to marriage than this."

4. *Practicing Responding in a Practice Group*

First, the parishioner, pastor, observer(s) (moderator and others) roles are assigned. Then the pastor attends and responds to the parishioner for five minutes (the moderator keeps the time). Next the moderator (observer) debriefs the parishioner, and then the pastor about the pastor's use of skills. Last, the moderator (and observers) gives the pastor feedback.

3

Assessing

might be true

THE ASSESSING SKILLS—the third and final subcluster of presence skills—
are used to detect the beliefs that participate in the key feelings and actions
that constitute parishioners' problems and joys. The three assessing skills
are summarizing, hunching, and eliciting. *Summarizing* pulls together the
relevant data from observing, listening, paraphrasing, and probing into a
succinct presentation of parishioners' views of situations. *Hunching* expresses intuitions about what is implied in parishioners' stories. *Eliciting*
uses probes to bring out the thoughts that lie behind parishioners' feelings
and actions.

Because the assessing skills focus on the underlying beliefs, they help
parishioners explore their concerns at a deeper level than do the responding
skills. Likewise they enable pastors to gain an advanced form of empathy—
an understanding of the values that form the basis of parishioners' perspectives on their experiences. Since these skills are built on the attending
and responding skills, pastors should have prepared a solid base of at least
several paraphrases (that parishioners have accepted) before they move to
assessing.

The assessing skills are used after the parishioners' exploration has led
them to focus on a central feeling or action. Pastors then bring this focus
to light through summarizing. If parishioners have indicated the thoughts
that go along with their feelings and actions then these are included in the
summary. If they have not, pastors help parishioners identify these beliefs
by hunching and eliciting. Thus, the assessing skills are transition skills.
They help parishioners move from exploring (stage 1) to understanding
(stage 2).

The following verbatim illustrates the use of assessing skills in the
context of a stage 1 conversation.

A PROBLEM WITH PRAYER

Patrick Wood, an active member of the congregation whose wife and son were killed in an automobile accident just over a year ago, comes to the pastor, Sandra Sherwood, during the coffee hour after worship.

Conversation

PATRICK: Pastor Sherwood, do you have a moment to talk?

SANDRA: Certainly.

PATRICK: Well, I don't know how to say this, but I . . . well, I guess I might as well come out and say it . . . I am not getting anything out of prayer.

SANDRA: Not getting anything?

PATRICK: I used to get a warm feeling every time I prayed. It was like God was right in the room with me, with his arms around me. It was wonderful . . . I felt so comforted. Now when I pray . . . nothing. No warm feeling, no sense of God. It's awful.

SANDRA: You feel bad because you no longer experience God's presence the way you used to.

PATRICK: Bad isn't the word for it. This last year has been a living hell. Please excuse me, pastor, but that's the truth. I have tried everything I know how to do. I read the pamphlets on prayer from the stand in the back of the church. I even went to a workshop on prayer. There I met some of the members of the prayer group who said that I would get help if I met with them. Well . . . I have been going to their prayer group for three months and I feel *worse* [*said with emphasis*] when I come from their meetings.

SANDRA: Worse?

PATRICK: Yes, worse! As you know, there are discussions at the end of the meetings, after we finish praying over the parish intercession list, where various members of the group talk about prayer. I had hoped to learn a lot from those discussions, but all they talk about is how close they feel to God. Every time I come from one of those meetings I feel worse about the fact that God isn't close to me anymore.

SANDRA: So, the meetings make you feel terrible. Instead of helping you solve the problem, they make you feel it more deeply.

PATRICK: Yes, that's right . . . Pastor, can you tell me a way to get that feeling again?

SANDRA: Well, I am certainly willing to talk with you about it. Let me see if I understand what you have said so far. This past year has been very painful for you because you have not been getting the good feeling that you used to get through praying. You have tried all the ways you know how to get it back but none have worked. In fact, exposure to the witness of some of the prayer group members has just increased the pain. Is that right?

PATRICK: Yes, that's about it—except that prayer is what I've needed to keep me going since Peg and John [his wife and son] were killed by that damned . . . excuse me . . . awful drunk driver thirteen months ago Tuesday.

SANDRA: You are frustrated because the one thing you desired after they died—prayer—has been taken away from you.

PATRICK: Yes, yes . . . you know I hadn't thought about it that way. Maybe their death and my feelings have something to do with my prayer problem.

SANDRA: How so?

PATRICK: I don't know . . . [*Pause*] Well maybe it was . . . I was so upset that God would let something like that happen to Peg and John. Peg was a good woman, you know that, pastor, she was one of the most active women in this church. And John was . . . was . . . was just a baby. [*He begins to tear*] Why would God let that happen? [*Said louder and more crisply*] It just doesn't seem right! I wish I knew who to be upset with because . . . you can't be mad with God . . . he . . . he wouldn't like it. Maybe that's why.

SANDRA: So you think that your difficulty with prayer may have something to do with your frustration with God over the unmerited deaths of your wife and baby.

PATRICK: Yes. [*Quietly*]

SANDRA: And these feelings are especially difficult because you believe that God wouldn't like your getting mad at God.

PATRICK: God wouldn't, would he?

SANDRA: I would like to respond to that question in a minute, but first, I would like to be certain where we are in the conversation. You have been having trouble with praying ever since your wife and son were killed by a drunk driver. You think that your difficulty in praying might be related to your not being able to express your anger because God wouldn't like it. And you would like to know more about how God feels about your anger.

PATRICK: Yes, that's it.

(The conversation moves to stage 2.)

Analysis

Because Patrick was having difficulty getting his story out, Sandra primed him with an accent. After Patrick responded to Sandra's probe, she paraphrased his answer. In response to the paraphrase, Patrick told more of the story. Picking up on the amount of feeling that accompanied the word "worse," Sandra repeated it, an accent. She was right; Patrick had a lot of feelings about the parish prayer group. Having just probed in the preceding interchange, Sandra paraphrased in this one. Patrick, sensing that his story had been told, asks for the pastor's opinion—thus inviting her into stage 2. The pastor accepts the invitation by offering a summary which ends with a request that Patrick accept or correct it. The parishioner accepts it, and then adds some other important information. (Note that parishioners frequently add other important information after a summary is offered for negotiation.) Then Sandra accepts the addition to the summary by paraphrasing it. Patrick accepts her paraphrase and uses it for insight into his feelings and their relationship to the problem. The pastor asks a short openended question to invite him to make his understanding of the relationship more explicit. Patrick's response includes a belief about God that keeps him from expressing his anger. Sandra highlights this belief in a paraphrase, which Patrick accepts. In response to Patrick's request for information about God's response to his anger, another invitation to stage 2, Sandra offers one last summary, which he affirms. In sum, Patrick has told his story, agreed on the pastor's understanding of it, and identified the belief that is blocking his ability to pray. Thus, pastor and parishioner are ready for the move from stage 1 to stage 2.

SUMMARIZING

Summarizing pulls together the relevant data from observing, listening, paraphrasing, and probing into a succinct presentation of parishioners' views of situations. In the verbatim above there are examples of two kinds of summaries, one without the assessment data and one with. Because Patrick had not indicated the beliefs that led to his frustration, Sandra could not include them in the first summary. These beliefs were included in the next summary, which prepared them to begin stage 2.

Primary Function

The most important use of summarizing is as a transition skill; it is used to provide closure for stage 1 exploring and to build the foundation for stage 2 understanding. When pastors think that they understand a situation enough to move a conversation to stage 2, they test this idea by offering a summary. This allows parishioners to verify or correct pastors' understandings. Much of pastors' authority to apply the gospel to parishioners' perceptions in stage 2 is based on their joint agreement, by means of a negotiated summary, on what those perceptions are.

Other Functions

Summaries are used in three other important ways: giving focus and movement to conversations, reopening a continued conversation, and including new participants in a conversation.

Focus conversations.   Summaries can give focus to a rambling conversation or movement to a stuck one. When parishioners are jumping from topic to topic or repeating the same information over and over, a summary can help provide focus and direction. Likewise, summaries are helpful in giving movement to conversations in which parishioners have gone as far as they can go on the subject. Imagine a rambling conversation during which a parishioner has been talking for a long time about a lot of things. The pastor might say, "Could you wait a moment while I see if I understand what you have said so far?" Then the pastor would offer a summary. Or, in a stuck conversation, a parishioner might say, "I just don't understand what is going on. I am totally confused." The pastor might respond, "Let's just review what you have said so far; maybe that will clarify things." Then the pastor would offer a summary.

Reopen continued conversations.   Summaries are a good way to reopen continued conversations. Pastoral conversations often begin with a short interchange on the telephone, after worship, or at a meeting during which a brief statement of the issue is given and an appointment is made for continuing the conversation. A summary of the previous interchange is a good way for the pastor to begin the subsequent conversation. For example, the pastor might begin the new conversation by saying, "If I remember correctly, you wanted to talk with me about the difficulties you were having with the way things are going in your family. You were feeling betrayed and confused by your wife's response to your son."

Involve new participants.   Summaries are also a helpful way to involve new participants in a continued conversation. The pastor may begin to talk with a new participant by summarizing, "Mr. Jones, your wife and I met briefly the other day. She told me how she felt about the way things were going between you. I told her that I needed to hear what you had to say before I could understand the situation. She agreed to ask you to come, and here we are."

Summarizing is the presence skill that pulls together all the information gained from attending and responding so that pastors and parishioners can better understand parishioners' feelings, actions, and thoughts related to their experiences. As such it focuses parishioners' previous exploration and provides a check on the pastors' empathy. Though it has other functions, summarizing is primarily the skill that begins the transition from stage 1 to stage 2.

HUNCHING

Hunching is expressing intuitions about what is implied in parishioners' stories. It is an advanced form of empathy that goes beyond interchangeable statements (paraphrasing) to offering considered guesses about what parishioners feel and mean. By sharing their hunches pastors invite parishioners to state fully those feelings and related beliefs that are implicit or partially expressed in their verbal and nonverbal messages. Communicating these feelings helps parishioners explore their issues more deeply.

Feeling Foolish

For example, the parishioner Jim is a seminary student who has been discussing his problems with another seminarian, Jessie. After using stage 1 skills for the first ten interchanges to help him examine these issues, Jessie offers a summary. She says, "As I understand it, you are upset because you can't seem to get your life together. In particular you are having trouble getting papers in on time, losing weight, and following your budget."

Jim replies, "Yeah. That's pretty much it." Because Jim accepted the summary, Jessie decides to share her hunch about his feelings in order to get him to express them more directly. She says, tentatively, "I wonder if you are upset with yourself about being in this situation."

Jim answers, "Sure, I'm upset! Wouldn't you be if you couldn't take care of a few simple things . . . If you had people bugging you and making fun of you all the time about not taking care of them . . . If you had to go to somebody and talk with them about your failures." Jim is speaking louder and more emphatically than previously, blurting the phrases out rapidly. He has responded by expressing his anger at himself for his weaknesses and his anger at others for reminding him of those weaknesses.

Jessie responds by paraphrasing to help him examine the feelings that the hunch brought up, saying, "You are very angry with yourself for having difficulties with these problems." Jim says, "I feel so stupid not being able to handle these things." Jessie replies, "Stupid?" Jim says, "Yeah, stupid. A failure! A fool, who can't deal with his own life, is trying to be a pastor so he can tell others how to handle theirs." Now that Jim expresses his feeling fully, Jessie offers a hunch about the belief that sustains this feeling, saying, "It seems like you're ashamed about having these problems because you believe that you should be able to take care of them without help." Jim accepts the hunch, saying, "That's right. I never thought of it quite like that, but that hits the nail right on the head."

Analysis

Hunching is based on the data gathered from attending and responding. Pastors develop hunches from two sources. First, pastors draw implications out of parishioners' statements and nonverbal behaviors by noticing patterns of feelings, experiences, actions, or thoughts and sharing hypotheses about them with parishioners. In the example above, Jessie's hunch about Jim being angry came out of careful attending to him. The second source for hunches is the pastors' knowledge of the type of beliefs that result in certain feelings. In the example, Jessie's hunch about Jim's underlying belief that he ought not have to accept help is partially based on his own statement and partially based on her understanding of the beliefs that underlie anger.

Hunches are guesses and therefore they are offered tentatively. For instance, both of the hunches in the conversation between Jessie and Jim illustrate tentativeness. In the first hunch, the tentativeness is in the tone and in the phrase "I'm wondering if . . ."; in the second, it is in the phrase "it seems like."

After hunches are offered, pastors then help parishioners explore their reactions. This enables parishioners to correct the ones they disagree with and digest the ones they affirm. In the conversation above, Jessie's paraphrase and accent helped Jim explore his response to her hunch.

Hunching is an important skill because it helps parishioners state their feelings and related beliefs more fully. This in turn helps them begin to see and understand the part that their perspective plays in their problems and joys. Thus, hunching is a bridge skill—it helps parishioners move from stage 1, exploring their problems and joys, to stage 2, understanding their part in those problems and joys.

ELICITING

Eliciting uses probes to bring out the thoughts that lie behind parishioners' feelings and actions. It is named as a separate skill from probing partly because it is only used in assessing and partly because it goes against several of the guidelines for probing. Eliciting does this by using questioning, sometimes sequentially, as the method of probing rather than employing the less intrusive ways.

Like summarizing and hunching, eliciting presupposes the knowledge and relationship-building activities of attending and responding. It is different from the other assessing skills in that the key feelings or actions that concern parishioners also need to be agreed upon before asking is appropriate. When these conditions have been met, then eliciting is a good way of aiding pastors and parishioners to discover the beliefs that underlie the feelings or actions in question. The following verbatim illustrates the use of eliciting in assessing.

A Marital Problem

Chester Nakamura, a pastor, and John Lee, a parishioner, have agreed that the behavior that John wants to explore is his difficulty in expressing his concerns to Jane, his wife. They have just finished exploring a particular situation in which John had this problem.

CHESTER: John, it is my experience that people usually think something before they do or refuse to do things. What thought came to you when you decided not to express your concern about the car to Jane?

JOHN: I don't know.

CHESTER. Think about it for a moment.

JOHN: [*Long pause*] I don't remember thinking of anything except that my stomach was getting tight.

CHESTER: Was there a rule or saying in your family that spoke against voicing negative feelings?

JOHN: [*Pause*] Oh, yeah. My dad always used to say, "If you can't say something good don't say anything at all."

CHESTER: That sounds like the kind of rule that could make it difficult for you to tell Jane that you didn't like the car she picked out.

JOHN: I knew she didn't want to hear any negative feedback and I didn't want to give it. I hadn't thought about that old saying for a while, but everybody in my family—especially my father and brothers—sure lives it. We never expressed much negative criticism to each other directly.

CHESTER: So the family rule, "If you can't say something good, don't say anything at all" may be the idea that keeps you from sharing your critiques with Jane.

JOHN: Yeah, I bet that's it.

Analysis

After establishing that John's action of refusing to communicate his negative feedback to Jane was the central concern, Chester asked about the thought that preceded the decision not to communicate. When John could not think of it, Chester asked again. When this form of eliciting didn't work, Chester tried a new strategy based on the fact that the belief was not conscious to John, since he did not remember it, but he did remember his stomach tightening. On that basis, Chester hypothesized that the thought might be a family rule since these are drummed into us so deeply that we often act on these beliefs without being conscious of them. Thus he asked about the family rule. Chester accepted John's answer because that rule was the type that often spawns a refusal to communicate negative feedback. The interchange continued with Chester reiterating this rule for confirmation and John responding in an affirming manner.

The skill of eliciting is that of searching for the underlying beliefs that are either upsetting parishioners or making them happy. Pointed questions can help parishioners identify unhelpful ideas. For example: What was it about that experience that so distressed you? What was so upsetting for you? What were you telling yourself during that experience? What is stopping you from responding the way you want? What keeps you continuing to act in the way you don't want? Chester's first question in the verbatim was a form of What were you telling yourself during that experience?

Helpful and Unhelpful Beliefs

The rule of thumb for discriminating between helpful and unhelpful beliefs is that beliefs that keep people feeling distressed or acting inappropriately contain some absolute "should" or "must" that demands their obedience and causes them to reject part of themselves, others, or the situation. In the example above the idea that he must not say anything negative kept John from communicating his concerns to his wife. By contrast, values that make people happy or respond creatively free them to accept themselves, others, and the situation.

When you are sure of parishioners' dominant distressing feelings then you have an idea of the form of must that is behind those feelings. This knowledge gives guidance to your eliciting. If the person is experiencing anxious dread, you might ask, "What is the 'must not happen' that frightens you?" Similarly, if despairing guilt is the issue, "What is the 'must do' or 'must not do' that you are violating?" When they are alienated from others the question is, "What is the 'must do' or 'must not do' that the other person(s) is transgressing?"

After parishioners identify a belief, it is important to help them explore it. This helps them understand and feel the relationship of the idea to their actions or feelings. In the verbatim above, Chester did this by repeating the rule expressed by John. This led to John's gradual affirmation of the rule's relationship to his relationship to Jane. Parishioners' understanding and experience of the contribution that thoughts make to emotions and behaviors are the necessary preparations for pastors' challenges to their ideas in stage 2.

Eliciting is the skill of inviting parishioners to name the thoughts that underlie their feelings and actions. It involves asking pointed questions about the ideas that parishioners have before or during the emotions or behaviors that are important to them. Like the other assessing skills, eliciting prepares parishioners to move from stage 1 to stage 2.

THE PRESENCE SKILLS— REVIEW AND PROBLEMS

The presence skills are designed to help parishioners carry out their task of exploration. Parishioners are helped by the attentiveness expressed by positioning, as well as by the data gathered through observing, listening, probing, and eliciting. These data are communicated to them by paraphrasing, summarizing, and hunching. These skills give parishioners and pastors the rich understanding of parishioners' feelings, experiences, actions, and thoughts that can lead to liberating understandings (stage 2) and effective actions (stage 3).

However, pastors and parishioners often find it difficult to stay in stage 1 because it can be uncomfortable. For example, it is unpleasant to carefully examine an unresolved problem when pastor and parishioner want to get things resolved. Similarly, it is tough for pastors to listen to parishioners' misunderstood experiences, ill-advised actions, or unhelpful thoughts without rushing to straighten them out. It is particularly painful to listen to and examine feelings of anger, anxiety, and guilt. Almost all mistakes in stage 1 are caused by pastors trying to avoid these discomforts by being *absent* from rather than *present* to parishioners.

Being Absent

Three common ways pastors are absent to parishioners are (1) focusing on self-expectations, (2) premature proclamations, and (3) instant solutions.

Self-expectation focus. Pastors are absent when they are focusing on self-expectations rather than on parishioners. They try so hard to do well that their attention is on themselves rather than on parishioners. Pastors focus on self-expectations because they think that they have to be good, wise, smart, or worthy to be helpful. The good news is that they can be helpful by simply being present.

Premature proclamations. Pastors are absent when they rush to share an insight before they have finished exploring the problem or joy with the parishioner. This is called premature proclamation. Pastors jump to these conclusions because they are paying attention to the problem, trying to figure it out, rather than being present to the person. In their haste to share insights, pastors forget that the relationship built through the presence skills is primary, and that pastors' insights are secondary. In the verbatim at the beginning of the chapter, Sandra had to fight the urge to prematurely correct Patrick's understanding of prayer and God's response to his anger. She waited until the tasks of stage 1 were completed with a summary.

Instant solutions. Instant solutions are strategies for solving the problems that are given before the pastor and parishioner have finished stage 1. Pastors give these in an effort to save the parishioner (and themselves) from the pain of having an unresolved problem. The wisdom of stage 1 (the wisdom of the cross) is that parishioners and pastors are helped by experiencing and exploring the pain of unresolved problems in the context of God's love. In the conversation between Sandra and Patrick, he asked for a solution early in the conversation, but Sandra continued the exploration by offering a summary that led them to discover the underlying beliefs that were blocking Patrick's prayer.

The presence skills are designed to keep pastors focused on parishioners—their feelings, experiences, actions, and thoughts—rather than on either themselves or parishioners' problems. This focus on parishioners communicates the empathy that is the pastors' best contribution to a helpful relationship.

LEARNING THE SKILLS

The assessing skills—summarizing, hunching, and eliciting—identify the beliefs that lie behind distressing feelings and actions. They are transition skills that (1) bring closure to stage 1 exploration by naming the unhelpful ideas, and (2) move the conversation toward stage 2 challenges of these thoughts. Pastors, in summarizing, offer parishioners succinct statements of parishioners' explorations, including any beliefs that they have stated. Hunching shares intuitions about implied feelings and beliefs to draw out both parishioners' major feelings and the beliefs that undergird those emotions. Eliciting questions parishioners as a way of discovering the beliefs that lie behind their feelings and actions. The material that is brought up by summarizing, hunching, and eliciting is then included in a more complete summary that identifies the beliefs that participate in parishioners' issues.

Exercises

1. Practicing Summarizing

A. Engage in a pastoral conversation in a practice group. After seven minutes of using presence skills offer a summary. Continue negotiating the summary until it is accepted. Reflect on the conversation with the parishioner and observer(s). Conclude by writing down your observations about summarizing.

B. Listen to a tape of your responding skills practice and write a summary of the parishioner's FEAT. Use that summary to begin your next conversation with that parishioner.

2. Practicing Hunching

A. Formulating hunches. Summarize a person's description of one of his or her problems or joys as in exercise 1A or 1B above. Develop a hunch about any key feelings or thoughts that were not fully expressed. Write your hunch in the form that you would share it. Evaluate your statement by the standards given in chapter 3.

3. *Practicing Eliciting*

Summarize a parishioner's description of the issue as in exercises 1 and 2. Then write a pointed question to elicit the belief that undergirds the parishioner's key behavior or feelings. Evaluate your statement by the standards given in chapter 3.

4. *Practicing the Presence Skills*

A. Practicing on your own issues. Begin by either choosing an issue to reflect upon or praying for discernment. After doing the one, do the other. Next, write down a description of the problem or joy as you see it. Then use the presence skills to help yourself explore this problem or joy as a dialogue between pastor and parishioner. Attending to your nonverbals, write your thoughts and feelings about the issue and respond with the responding skills. Finish by assessing the beliefs that are implicit in your "parishioner" responses.

After you have finished writing your dialogue, reflect on it by answering these questions in writing: How do I feel about the problem or joy after doing this exercise? What insights have I gained or deepened by doing this?

Conclude by checking your "pastor" responses against the standards for each skill in chapter 3 and the review of the presence skills (pp. 54–56). Write down the insights you gained about your use of the presence skills.

B. Practicing presence skills in a practice group. Engage in a pastoral conversation in a practice group. After seven minutes (moderator signals time to pastor) offer a summary for negotiation. After a summary is accepted, use hunching or eliciting to get at the beliefs that sustain the feelings or behaviors that are central for the parishioners. Offer a final summary that includes these beliefs. Reflect on the conversation with the parishioners and observers. Conclude by writing down your observations about the presence skills.

PART TWO

INTERVENTIONS

4
Theological Assessment

THIS CHAPTER PROVIDES the theoretical bridge between the discussions of the presence skills and the proclamation skills. Its purpose is to introduce the theological thinking that evaluates the ideas identified through assessing (chap. 3) and formulates the theological arguments used in proclamation (chap. 5).

Theological assessment is the art of thinking theologically about the beliefs that undergird parishioners' feelings and actions. *Theological disputation* is the process of teaching the good news and challenging nongospel beliefs. Although the quality of the pastoral relationship, stressed in the discussion of the presence skills, is a foundational means of communicating the gospel, nonetheless providing a theological perspective is the unique contribution of pastors. Theological assessment and disputation are the methods of providing a theological perspective.

Theological assessment and disputation aid both pastors and parishioners. These skills help parishioners cope by making sense of their experiences through relating them to their religious faith and practices. They give pastors direction by indicating the beliefs that should be challenged or celebrated and the ways to argue with or affirm them. In addition, assessment and disputation point to the religious resources that may be needed. We can see the role of these arts by looking again at the pastoral conversation reported in the Introduction.

REVISITING THE HOSPITAL
Stage 1: Exploring

Chris opened the conversation with a greeting and then asked Martha how she was feeling. Martha responded by complaining about being hospitalized. Chris drew out Martha's concerns by paraphrasing her thoughts and feelings. It soon became evident to both of them that Martha's chief issue was worry about her children's welfare during her hospitalization. Her key statement was made with great emotion, "I just don't think my husband can take care of the children the same way that I do, and I know that I shouldn't worry about it so much—but I do."

Chris, the pastor, noted that anxiety is primary and that there is a secondary guilt about her anxious feelings. After Martha's key statement Chris probed carefully to see if she was worried because her husband had some pattern of neglect, abuse, or gross incompetence in handling the children. Since the parishioner's central issue was anxiety, the pastor probed to determine the reality base for her concern. When Martha convinced her that this was not the issue, Chris summarized her concerns by stating, "It seems to me that the most uncomfortable thing about being in the hospital is your constant worry about the children not getting the proper care from your husband. You feel guilty, also, about worrying so much because he does love them and can take care of them. Is that right?"

By making this summary the pastor further tested the accuracy of her assessment of worry and despair. Martha confirmed Chris's summary. Noting that the feelings were clear but the ideas that undergird the feelings were not fully stated, Chris followed the summary with a hunch. Then Chris said, "I wonder if you believe that a good Christian must not be anxious?" Martha replied, "Yes, I guess I do. My mother always quoted that Scripture, 'Be ye not anxious,' and I guess it stuck with me that anxiety is wrong." After paraphrasing Martha's statement Chris asked her what thought made her so anxious regarding the children. Now that the idea behind the guilt has been surfaced, Chris tried to elicit the idea behind the anxiety. After some prompting Martha said, "I just keep thinking that it would be a catastrophe if something happened to them and I wasn't there." Chris then offered another summary that included the beliefs that lay behind Martha's guilt and anxiety. Now that Chris had used assessing skills to identify the beliefs associated with both Martha's anxiety and her guilt, the process of exploring was completed and they were ready to move to stage 2.

Stage 2: Understanding

Chris addressed Martha's worry and embarrassment by reminding Martha about how worried Chris had been about leaving the parish in Martha's care during her sabbatical. Chris then asked Martha if she remembered her own advice to Chris. After a pause, Martha smiled and replied, "I told you that you needed to learn to trust us, and that you needed to turn the parish over to God in prayer." Martha's smile got broader and she continued, "You certainly play dirty, reminding me of what I said." Then they had a good laugh together.

The laughter helped Martha feel less guilty and less anxious. It freed her to decide that she wanted to stop worrying so much about the kids. After making a theological assessment that the parishioner was blocked by worry and despair, the pastor challenged her to face her part in creating these feelings by asking a question that implied that Martha was making herself worry more than necessary in this situation in the same way that Martha indicated that Chris had been doing before the sabbatical. Chris also challenged Martha's guilt about her dread by getting her to remember a situation in which Chris, an ordained person, was anxious. Both Martha's acceptance of these challenges and her change of perspective were indicated by her laughter.

Stage 3: Acting

Martha asked Chris, "What enabled you to stop bugging me after I gave you the advice to turn it over? How did you turn the parish over to God?" Chris answered, "I worked out this plan to pray for you and the church board for fifteen minutes at the beginning of each day. After a week or so of doing this, I calmed down." Martha thought about this answer for awhile and decided to pray for her children and husband whenever she woke up either in the morning or during the day. At Chris's suggestion, she agreed to keep a record of this praying so that they could discuss it during her next visit. Chris pushed the conversation toward closure by asking Martha to review the plan; when she did this accurately, Chris decided that she was ready to implement it. They prayed together with Chris acknowledging Martha's anxiety and guilt before God and then putting these feelings in the context of scriptural images of God's power and forgiveness. Then Chris said good-bye and left.

Thus, the pastor and Martha developed a plan to deal with the primary problem identified by theological assessment—dread—by using a religious resource—prayer. Chris also used a closing prayer as a resource to help Martha resolve her despair and dread through consciousness of God's forgiveness and power. The focus on prayer is a response to the theological assessment of anxiety and guilt.

This example shows how theological assessment and disputation organize a pastoral conversation. In stage 1 Martha and Chris worked on gathering the data to make a theological assessment. Chris then, in stage 2, disputed the beliefs identified as unhelpful by that assessment. Last,

Martha and Chris developed a stage 3 plan to further dispute the unhelpful ideas.

BELIEFS AND THE GOSPEL

The importance of beliefs in communicating the gospel can be seen in the conversation reported above. Martha's experience of God's presence, power, and forgiveness was blocked by beliefs that left her anxious and despairing about her worry. When Chris challenged these beliefs, Martha was able to experience enough of God's forgiveness and hope to begin to change her behavior. The communication of the gospel through the pastoral relationship was fundamental because it allowed Martha to be challenged to feel both her despair and Chris's absolution. The challenge of her beliefs further opened her to the experience of the good news.

Scripture

The importance of correct beliefs about God for opening one to experience God's presence and power is the constant witness of Scripture. The Ten Commandments emphasize the importance of a correct understanding of God by devoting the vast majority of the words to the first four commandments about God, leaving a few terse verses to the final six commandments that guide our relations to neighbors (Exod. 20:1-17; Deut. 5:6-21). The stories of the kings of Israel tell us that Israel's success depended on the worship of the true God and the rejection of idolatry (1 and 2 Samuel, 1 and 2 Kings, 1 and 2 Chronicles). The major and minor prophets each in his own way warn Israel against the idolatry practiced by other peoples, and urge their own people to change their beliefs (with the resulting changes in behavior) about God. In sum, the Hebrew Scriptures are one continuous challenge to idolatry and wrong understandings of God that lead to unjust behavior and societal collapse.

In the New Testament Jesus continues the prophets' ministry by contending with the subtle idolatry expressed by the false beliefs of those who purport to worship the true God. The Synoptic Gospels recall that the center of Jesus' ministry was the call to repentance (*metanoia*) (Mark 1:15, Matt. 4:17, Luke 5:32). Jesus devoted his ministry to teaching and illustrating a correct understanding of God. The New Testament also records that Jesus' followers continued this emphasis on the right understanding of God: they taught, preached, wrote letters, and lived in model ways in order to combat idolatry and help people accept the gospel's life-giving understanding of God.

Idolatry

Thomas Oden (1969) has shown the relation of idolatry to our basic problematic feelings. He offers an existential analysis of human relationships to time, self, others, God, and nature and concludes that the basic problem with the past is guilt, with the future, anxiety, and with the present, boredom. The problems with self, others, God, and nature can be summarized as alienation. He then notes theologically that guilt cannot persist before God whose nature is forgiveness. Anxiety is needless before God who owns the future; boredom and alienation disappear before God who enlivens the present with both the invitation and power to love. Oden concludes that since God provides the answer to guilt, anxiety, boredom, and alienation the persistence of these distressing feelings is the result of our clinging to idols—making lesser values our ruling values.

In the conversation between Chris and Martha, Martha was stuck in despair over transgressing her value that a good Christian must not be anxious. She despaired because that value was so important that she was not accepting God's gift of unmerited forgiveness. In this situation the value was an idol because it, not God's love and forgiveness, was central to her sense of self-worth. As an important value the injunction "Be ye not anxious" motivated her to turn things over to God; as a ruling value it kept her guilty because she failed to trust God in this situation—a fact that could not be undone. Chris, her pastor, communicated the gospel to her by challenging the belief that her self-worth depended on the shifting sands of ethical performance and by helping her place it on the solid rock of God's love and forgiveness. Chris did this by sharing that she, a Christian designated as a model by virtue of her ordination, had suffered a similar transgression; and she said this in a way that communicated her own acceptance of God's forgiveness.

Oden's theological assertion that idolatry is the source of persistent guilt, anxiety, boredom, and alienation provides a contemporary application of the biblical insights that idolatry is the central human problem. It shows that incorrect beliefs interfere with the appreciation of God's power, forgiveness, and empowering invitation to love. Oden's understanding provides the basic theological rationale for the theological assessment categories of guilt, anxiety, and anger (my term for his boredom and alienation) which are discussed in this chapter.

RATIONAL-EMOTIVE THERAPY

Rational-emotive therapy (RET), developed by Albert Ellis (1962), maintains that the best way to help people change feelings and behaviors is to help them replace unhelpful beliefs with helpful beliefs. Ellis's understanding provides the psychological application for Oden's theological assertion. In this section we consider three key formulations of RET: the ABC Theory, the irrational beliefs, and disputation and effect.

ABC Theory

Ellis presents his cognitive theory of the relation of thoughts to emotions and behavior in an A-B-C form: A = activating experience, B = belief about that experience, and C = consequences (emotional or behavioral) that take place. He maintains that B (the belief about A) causes C (1974, 55–68). To illustrate: A (the activating experience)—John Smith receives a grade of C in church history; B (belief system)—John believes that he must not get C's because he must get at least a B or he is no good; he believes, also, that it is right that he is down on himself because a worthwhile seminarian would not make a C; and he hates the teacher for giving the C; the C (consequence)—John is depressed. Ellis would argue that John is depressed because of his irrational belief that performance measures self-worth. He would back up this point of view by noting that Mary Jones also got a C but she is not depressed, just disappointed. Mary held the rational belief that the grade of C indicated no more than that she did not fully satisfy Professor Brown's expectations on the two examinations. John, because he is depressed, finds it difficult either to enjoy himself or to study. Because Mary is disappointed, not depressed, she uses the C to motivate her to clarify and understand better both instructors' expectations and her own abilities.

Ellis (1962, 35–39) maintains that replacing beliefs is the best way to change feelings and behaviors. However, it is not the only way. Other methods include stimulating the hypothalamus and the automatic nervous system through electricity and drugs and working on the sensorimotor systems through various types of exercises (e.g., relaxation, dancing, screaming, etc.). The RET method has the advantage of being more widely applicable and more under parishioners' control than the other methods mentioned here.

Thus, the ABC theory is extremely useful for theological assessment because it rediscovers and puts in the context of contemporary psychological research the scriptural wisdom (e.g., Rom. 12:2, Eph. 4:23) that beliefs are very important in determining feelings and behavior.

Ten Irrational Beliefs

Ellis has identified a number of beliefs that cause people to reject the reality of situations, function poorly, and be stuck in painful emotions such as anxiety, guilt, and anger. He calls these "irrational beliefs." Below are the titles for ten of Ellis's statements of irrational belief, which I have adapted from those developed by Jones (1968).

Demand for Approval
High Self-expectations
Condemning the Offender
Low Frustration Tolerance
Emotional Irresponsibility
Anxious Overconcern
Problem Avoidance
Historical Determinism
Need for Perfection
Passive Happiness

Disputation and Effect

The RET cognitive method of helping John Smith would be to help him to dispute his irrational beliefs. John would be challenged to produce the evidence that a C in church history makes him worthless (high self-expectations), that it is right to be down on himself for getting a C (condemning the offender), and that he should not forgive Professor Brown (condemning the offender). He would be challenged further to consider the evidence that none of the beliefs is true. Thus, the rational-emotive therapist would dispute John's irrational beliefs, teach John to dispute them, and give John homework in which he would practice disputing these beliefs by reason, actions, imagery, and so on, until John attained the desired effect—to end John's depression.

With the disputation and the effect included in the description of Ellis's theory, the essentials of rational emotional therapy expand from ABC to ABCDE (activating experience, belief, consequence, disputation, and effect).

Ellis's disputation and effect treatment is helpful in determining the agenda for stages 2 and 3. In the second (proclamation) stage the pastor disputes the unhelpful beliefs of the parishioner. The parishioner and pastor design a plan for the parishioner to continue disputing these beliefs as part of stage 3.

I relate Ellis to Oden by thinking of the irrational ideas as idols. For example, John's high self-expectations—"The idea that you *must* prove thoroughly competent, adequate, and achieving"—in the example above is a good value used idolatrously. Expecting oneself to be competent is worthwhile because it motivates one to do the good work that supports positive self-worth. The *must,* however, changes it from a worthwhile value to a ruling value (an idol). As an idol high self-expectations destroys self-worth because one is never totally competent in any situation and there are always situations in which one is not competent at all.

My primary reason for using RET is that it is a well-researched, widely used, and effective modern psychotherapeutic system that focuses on beliefs as the key to distressing feelings and behaviors (Ellis, 1977). Other theories place the basic problem elsewhere: unconscious conflicts (psychoanalytic), blocked growth (humanistic), maladaptive behavior (behaviorist), dysfunctional systems (family systems), oppression (radical), thinking errors (other cognitive theories), and physiological factors (medical). Each of these systems has proved helpful to some (Frank, 1974). In addition, Clinebell (1981) has shown that the insights and practices of each of these systems can be applied to communicating the gospel. No one of these theories, however, treats beliefs as seriously as does RET. Since the proclaiming and correcting of beliefs is basic to the lay and ordained roles of teaching, preaching, and giving theological and ethical counsel, pastors need a way of understanding human behavior that highlights the importance of the beliefs.

A second reason for using RET is that it adapts readily to the brief problem management counseling that is appropriate for use by lay persons, seminarians, and nonspecialist clergy. Many of the systems listed in the previous paragraph require extensive training for the pastor, and long-term counseling for the parishioner. In addition, RET's basic concepts are easily remembered and applied, an important advantage for nonspecialists.

With this summary of Ellis's contributions we are now ready to discuss the three theological assessment categories—guilt, anxiety, and anger— which employ the RET theory of change and ten irrational beliefs in service of Oden's theological analysis. Each of the following assessment categories is rich in concepts. Therefore, there is an exercise after each category to help you digest it before you attempt to take in more.

GUILT

Guilt is the state of having transgressed values that are important to our relationships with ourselves, others, and God. Guilt is universal because finitude, weakness, and selfishness continually involve us in doing those things we ought not to do and leaving undone those things that we ought to do. These transgressions give rise to guilt feelings that might or might not be conscious. These feelings are important because they give us direction by helping us not to do things that will damage our sense of self-worth, our relationships with others, or our relationship to God. Guilt feelings also spur us to make restitution and seek reconciliation when damage has occurred. Thus the purpose of guilt feelings is to motivate us to develop our abilities to be responsible in our relationships.

Acceptance and Despair

Acceptance and despair are the opposite responses to the phenomenon of guilt. When we allow the guilt to move us to seek reconciliation with God, neighbor, and ourselves we discover that God's mercy, which exceeds anything we can ask for or imagine, has preceded and inspired our search. We find that we are accepted. Acceptance is the trust in God's forgiveness that frees us to affirm our past despite sins, failures, limitations, and weaknesses. Martha experienced some of this acceptance when Chris reminded her that she had been anxious in the same way that Martha was. Because Chris's witness undermined Martha's high self-expectations she no longer felt alone and unacceptable because she was anxious. This new sense of acceptance freed her to want to work on her anxiety.

By contrast, when we continue to focus on our and others' past sins, failures, limitations, and weaknesses we fall into despair. Despair is the low self-esteem, shame, and blaming self and others that comes from not accepting God's mercy. Despair takes away the energy for change. Jude's pep talk, consisting of reasons that Martha should not be anxious, served to reinforce her belief that she must not worry. Because he reinforced Martha's high self-expectations, Jude's visit resulted in Martha becoming more deeply mired in despair.

Irrational Beliefs

The irrational beliefs that sustain despair are all ideas that emphasize impossible *musts*. Three of those that Hauck (1973) and Daly & Burton (1983) link with despair and depression are:

Demand for approval. Demand for approval is the idea that you must have love or approval from all the people you find significant. This belief takes a good value, seeking approval, and makes it an ultimate value, the one thing one must have. Thus when we try to earn self-worth by engaging in the impossible project of trying to get everyone's approval, we doom ourselves to failure and the consequent lowering of self-worth. In addition, we usually pay the price of abandoning some of our own values in order to gain approval from others; this costs us our self-approval and thus further lowers our sense of self-worth. By contrast the Christian gospel tells us that the approval we need is an unconditional gift from God (Rom. 5:1-11)—our self-worth is assured.

High self-expectations.   High self-expectations is the idea that you must prove thoroughly competent, adequate, and achieving.

This belief takes an important value, striving for competence, and makes it ultimate. The goal of being thoroughly competent is impossible to reach because we are by nature limited in attitude, knowledge, and skill. The striving for total competence leads to despair for two reasons: (1) we are destined to fail and (2) we are distracted from enjoying the competencies we do have. The Christian gospel comforts us with the promise that we are justified (given worth by God) as a free gift, despite not living up to the law (Rom. 3:21-31). This good news guarantees our self-worth.

Condemning the offender.   One condemns the offender when one blames or damns people (including yourself) who act obnoxiously and unfairly, seeing them as bad, wicked, or rotten individuals.

Holding ourselves and others accountable for actions is an important value. Condemning the offender takes this value and uses it to destroy the God-given worth of persons. When we blame, we make concern for our wishes, an important value, the center of the world; the creature takes the place of the Creator. Second, blaming others turns our attention from our issues to other's faults, thus diverting our energies from the esteem-building task of dealing with our problems. Finally, condemning others for their weaknesses makes us less able to accept our own. Thus it increases our despair.

The good news is that Christ is the Judge of the living and the dead (1 Pet. 4:5) and he showed his love for all in dying for our sins (1 Pet. 3:18)—"while we were yet sinners Christ died for us" (Rom. 5:8). Christ instructs us to judge not that we not be judged and to forgive as we have been forgiven (Luke 6:37). By not judging others we are released from the burden of establishing our self-worth by meeting the standards we use to judge others. Instead, we rejoice that our worth and theirs has been won by Christ.

Evaluating Guilt

The guilt category helps pastors evaluate parishioners' responses to their transgressions. Do they sink into despair based on beliefs such as the demand for approval, high self-expectations, and condemning the offender? Or do they admit their faults, trust in God's forgiveness, and therefore experience the freeing power of acceptance?

The following exercise is designed to help you increase your understanding of the guilt category. It may take some time to remember an issue and reread portions of the preceding section, and conceive of arguments in order to do the exercise, but it is important to do so because everything else in the model depends on your having a good grasp on the theological assessment categories.

Exercise

1. Think of an issue of yours in which guilt is the core theological issue and despair is the subcategory. List the feelings that help you to identify the issue as guilt (see the exercise section at the end of chapter 2 for a list of feelings related to guilt). Write down the thoughts or ideas that sustain those feelings. Then determine and record the irrational beliefs to which your beliefs are related.
2. Which, if any, of the arguments against the irrational beliefs (that you recorded in 1. above) did you find convincing and helpful? What arguments from Scripture, tradition, reason, or experience would you add to or substitute for those?

ANXIETY

Anxiety is a fearful response to real or imagined future threats to that which we value. Two human traits are the ability to imagine the future and the inability to protect that which we value against all threats. Thus anxiety is common to us all. Anxiety, like guilt, is important; it motivates us to both protect ourselves against the anticipated threat and turn to God.

Hope and Dread

Hope and dread are two alternative ways to respond to anxiety. *Hope* is trust in God's loving power that frees us to face the future—in spite of the fact that we cannot control it. Hope is not to be confused with simple optimism, which is the belief that things will work out the way we want them. Hope is the belief that things are all right, even though they may not work out the way we want. Simple optimism is the denial of anxiety, whereas hope is anxiety transformed through facing and accepting fear, putting trust in God, letting go of that which is threatened, and then engaging in an appropriate response.

Martha experienced hope when Chris reminded her of her own advice to Chris. The fact that what Martha had said in that situation was important enough for Chris to remember and value reminded Martha that God had given her the strength and wisdom to deal with a difficult situation in the past. This gave her hope for the future. Her knowledge that Chris was able to follow that advice with good result stopped her from feeling so desperate—she knew there was something that could be done. Though she still felt anxious, she was hopeful enough to have the energy to work out a plan.

Dread is terror in the face of powerlessness and death that comes from trusting in those things that pass away. Instead of trusting in God, who is the only permanent value, the worrier either focuses on the threat or seeks security in some method of avoiding the threat. The result of dread is the inability to engage in the appropriate response to the threat. One either acts frantically or avoids responding—two symptoms of hopelessness.

After Jude's visit Martha had less hope that she would be able to deal with her anxiety. Jude had not listened to Martha's anxiety but had shifted the conversation to his own agenda. Thus Martha had not been given a chance to break the power of the anxiety by sharing it. Instead, Jude's avoidance of her feelings had confirmed her deep fears that they were too frightening to manage.

Irrational Beliefs

The irrational beliefs that lie behind dread are various forms of catastrophizing—focusing on what *must* not happen. Three ideas that are connected with dread in Hauck's (1975) and Zwemer and Deffenbacher's (1984) work are:

Anxious overconcern.   Anxious overconcern is when something seems dangerous or fearsome, you must preoccupy yourself with it and make yourself anxious about it.

This belief takes the positive value of alertness to possible threats and intensifies it until it becomes central in one's consciousness (an idol). Anxious overconcern is unhelpful because it makes forming an objective evaluation of the threat and taking appropriate steps much harder. By making the threat central, worry exaggerates its danger. Likewise, worry makes it difficult to resign oneself to things that cannot be changed.

The gospel message counsels us not to be anxious because God takes care of the birds and clothes the grass and therefore will take care of us (Matt. 6:25-32). Instead of worrying we are to "strive first for the kingdom of God and his righteousness, and all these things will be given to you as well" (Matt. 6:33).

Problem avoidance. Problem avoidance is the idea that one can more easily avoid facing many life difficulties and self-responsibilities than undertake more rewarding forms of self-discipline.

This belief takes the good value of not worrying about a task until the proper time comes and makes the "not worrying" a central value by avoiding the task altogether. This does not work because avoidance of a task usually leads to further problems, and avoidance undermines our skill in facing anxiety, thus increasing the tendency to dread.

Passive happiness. The idea of passive happiness is similar to problem avoidance. One thinks that one can achieve maximum human happiness by inertia and inaction or by passively and uncommittedly enjoying oneself.

The important value of rest and enjoyment is made a central value negating the importance of exertion and commitment. As a ruling value it is untrue because humans require deep involvement in some activity to stay really alive and happy. Thus humans who resist this involvement are usually defending themselves (consciously or unconsciously) against some dread such as fear of failure. These fears can only be conquered by involvement and action.

The gospel message that speaks to both of these beliefs is Jesus' teaching that those who would save their lives, lose them, and those who lose their lives for his sake and the gospel will save them (Mark 8:34-35 and parallels).

Feeling Secure

These three beliefs—anxious overconcern, problem avoidance, and passive happiness—are idolatrous because they lead persons to put their energy into the impossible project of making insecure lives, values, and plans secure by worrying, avoiding, or alibiing. For example, two prevalent worries related to irrational beliefs are that someone will not approve or that you will not be thoroughly competent. Both of these worries are bound to come true; thus, fearing the possibility of their coming true is a waste of energy.

Christian beliefs, by contrast, lead persons to put their trust in the only one who is secure—God. The difference in the two belief systems is highlighted by the Christian understanding, expressed dramatically in the apocalyptic portions of the New Testament, that Christ comes and will come precisely when human lives, values, and plans, as well as the whole created order, are turned upside down (cf. Mark 13 and parallels, also Revelation 4–22). Thus the realization of our worst fears is transformed into a herald of our fondest hope. The acceptance of God as Creator and Consummator of the world frees creatures to face the future with a hope that manifests itself in productivity and creativity.

Evaluating Anxiety

The assessment category of anxiety helps pastors think about parishioners' responses to threat. Do they respond with dread or hope? Beliefs such as anxious overconcern, problem avoidance, and passive happiness usually undergird dread. Christian hope is based on trust in God's loving power, which is stronger than death.

The following exercise is designed to help you increase your understanding of the anxiety category to the level you will need in order to use the metanoia model in pastoral conversations. Please stop and do the exercise before continuing reading.

Exercise

1. Think of an issue of yours in which anxiety is the core theological issue and dread is the subcategory. List the feelings that help you to identify the issue as anxiety (see the exercise section at the end of chapter 2 for a list of feelings related to anxiety). Write down the thoughts or ideas that sustain those feelings. Then determine and record the irrational beliefs to which your beliefs are related.
2. Which, if any, of the arguments against the irrational beliefs (that you recorded in 1. above) did you find convincing and helpful? What arguments from scripture, tradition, reason, or experience would you add to or substitute for those?

ANGER

Anger is the frustrated response to past disappointments, future risks, and present obstacles that interfere with our expressing care for others. Caring always exposes us to disappointments since all persons transgress their and our values at one time or another. Likewise, caring is always risky since involvement exposes us to threats to the relationship and to that part of us which is invested in it. In addition, there are present obstacles to the relationship that are part of the limits and weaknesses of us, the other, and the environment. Therefore, caring continually exposes us to frustrating elements that anger us. Anger is important because it gives us energy and direction for meeting our need to care by expanding our ability to love.

Love and Alienation

Love and alienation are opposite reactions to the costliness of practicing the basic human instinct to care. In the following discussion, *love* is a general term used to include all grades of care, affection, and service. *Alienation* includes boredom, envy, hurt, hostility, jealousy, resentment, and sadness.

Love is care liberated to serve by God's acceptance and power—in spite of past disappointments, future risks, and present obstacles. Love is the fruit of experiencing God's acceptance and loving power. These experiences of God transform our natural caring, which is somewhat dependent on good feelings and promising circumstances, into love that can withstand bad feelings and frightening circumstances. Though affection is the basis of natural caring, Christian love includes the components of will and behavior; thus we are often called to decide (will) to act (behavior) in a loving way even though we do not feel affectionate at the time.

In the example of Chris's visit to Martha, Chris showed love by listening to Martha's feelings, waiting until an appropriate time to share her own weaknesses in order to help Martha feel accepted, and sharing her plan when asked but not forcing the plan on Martha. Chris disciplined her natural caring for Martha through using the pastoral skills.

Alienation is care deformed into self-protection by dread of the future, despair over the past, and dissatisfaction in the present. Alienation's connection to despair and dread is that the angers that block care are often either disguised dread or projected despair. The classic example of disguised fear as anger is the bullying behavior of a person who is afraid of others. Thus alienation is often used as a mask for dread by those who are unwilling to admit their fear directly. A comparable example of projection (to see and respond to something in others which we do not acknowledge in ourselves) is the oversensitivity to the aggressiveness of others by those who do not realize how aggressive they themselves are.

Alienation, the refusal or inability to risk care, shows in the withdrawal from self and neighbor through either aggressive or passive behavior. Aggressive behavior is characterized by striking out rather than reaching out; preoccupation with the need to protect oneself results in stifling one's need to care for the other. Passive behavior shows itself as holding back instead of reaching out; it is an attempt to avoid either causing hurt to others or being frustrated ourselves. With either aggressive or passive behavior neither person's needs are met. Our deepest needs are met when we engage in the empowering service which is love.

Jude, Martha's first visitor in the example in the Introduction, illustrated his alienation by focusing on his own frustrations with doctors, nurses, volunteers, and the billing department of the hospital instead of listening to Martha's feelings. Perhaps his alienation was related to his unresolved frustration or perhaps it was his way of withdrawing from Martha's anxiety. Whatever the reason, Jude was absent from Martha and focused on condemning the offenders.

Irrational Beliefs

Beliefs that sustain alienation are all some form of making the situation seem awful (Ellis calls this "awfulizing") by thinking that others *must* not do certain things.

Condemning the offender.   The central irrational belief that alienation shares with despair is condemning the offender. This is the idea that when people (including yourself) act obnoxiously and unfairly, you should blame or damn them, and see them as bad, wicked, or rotten individuals. Holding others accountable is helpful to them and us. It supports them in their desire to act responsibly and it allows us to care for them by providing that support. Blaming, however, does not aid either. It demands that the other must never be mistaken, irresponsible, mean, or different from what we want them to be—an impossible requirement for them to meet. First and foremost, condemnation makes the mistake of judging the person's whole worth on the basis of the behaviors that you dislike. Second, blaming others focuses our attention on their faults, thus making it more difficult to meet our need to respect and care for them. Last, blaming is an ineffective strategy because others tend to respond defensively to blame, rather than correct their behavior.

In opposition to blaming, Jesus in John's Gospel commands us to love one another (15:12), illustrates this love by laying down his life for us (15:13), promises that if we abide in him and follow his commandment we will bear fruit (15:16), and prays that the Father's love may be in us (17:26). The connection between accepting others and accepting oneself is classically stated in the Lord's Prayer (Our Father), "Forgive us our sins as we forgive those who sin against us" (ICET text; cf. Matt. 6:12, 14-15; Luke 11:4).

Two additional irrational beliefs lie behind alienation, in addition to those that lie behind dread and despair: low frustration tolerance and need for perfection.

Low frustration tolerance. The idea that you have to view things as awful, terrible, horrible, and catastrophic when you get seriously frustrated, treated unfairly, or rejected indicates a low frustration tolerance.

The important value of caring about ourselves and our plans becomes a ruling value of caring when one chooses to see frustration, unfair treatment, and rejection as intolerable. It is unhelpful as a central value for the following reasons: We have a choice not to see things as a disaster; thus we make ourselves angry. Further, when we make ourselves very upset, we will almost invariably block ourselves from taking effective action. Finally, reacting this way makes it more difficult to learn to accept things we cannot change.

The Beatitudes teach that being seriously frustrated, treated unfairly, and rejected can be paths to the kingdom (Luke 6:20-31; Matt. 5:1-12). For instance, "Blessed are you when people hate you, and when they exclude you, revile you, and defame you on account of the Son of Man. Rejoice in that day and leap for joy, surely your reward is great in heaven; for that is what their ancestors did to the prophets" (Luke 6:22-23; cf. Matt. 5:12).

Need for perfection. That people and things should turn out better than they do and that one must view it as awful and horrible if one does not find good solutions to life's grim realities is the need for perfection.

This belief takes the helpful value of trying to do things well and makes it a ruling value by construing it as catastrophic if things do not go exactly as we think they should. This is not a helpful belief because: (1) no good reason exists that things must be the way we want them; (2) usually the major effect that others have by not acting the way we would like is caused by our thinking that it affects us; (3) worrying about what they do sidetracks us from dealing with our legitimate concern, the way we behave; (4) searching for the nonexistent absolutely right solution distracts us from seeing the many viable, though imperfect, solutions that are available. In sum, the demand for perfection always leaves us frustrated. It alienates us from reality which contains imperfect situations, imperfect others, and our imperfect selves.

In direct contrast to our perfectionistic demand that things be different, the New Testament epistles exhort us: "Give thanks in all circumstances" (1 Thess. 5:18a), ". . . giving thanks to God the Father at all times . . ." (Eph. 5:20), ". . . with thanksgiving let your requests be made known to God" (Phil. 4:6). Giving thanks enables us to: (1) intensify our experiences of God's gifts of unmerited acceptance and hope; (2) put our frustrations in perspective by emphasizing God's grace and power; (3) enjoy that which can be enjoyed; (4) neutralize the rage that keeps us from seeing and engaging the viable alternatives.

Valuing Forgiveness

These three irrational beliefs—condemning the offender, low frustration tolerance, and need for perfection—are idolatrous as a group because they lead to the worship of the values of moral perfection and self-protection rather than to the worship of the God who values forgiveness and self-giving. Thus, this idolatrous worship frustrates the human need to care by making those who lack moral perfection and those who are risky to care for unfit to care about. This way of living is in direct contrast with the gospel, which calls us to love in spite of others' imperfections and our risks, thus freeing us to care for others.

The assessment category of anger is designed to help pastors reflect on parishioners' responses to the frustration of their caring. The two alternative responses are alienation and love. Alienation is based on beliefs such as: condemning the offender, low frustration tolerance, and the need for perfection. It is often a cover-up for dread or despair. Love is care liberated to serve by God's acceptance and power; it is undergirded by beliefs that sustain acceptance and hope.

The following exercise is designed to help you increase your understanding of the anger category. It is important to do this exercise for the reasons given for the previous two.

Exercise

1. Think of an issue of yours in which anger is the core theological issue and alienation is the subcategory. List the feelings that help you to identify the issue as anger (see the exercise section at the end of chapter 2 for a list of feelings related to anger). Write down the thoughts or ideas that sustain those feelings. Then determine and record the irrational beliefs to which your beliefs are related.

2. Which, if any, of the arguments against the irrational beliefs (that you recorded in 1. above) did you find convincing and helpful? What arguments from Scripture, tradition, reason, or experience would you add to or substitute for those?

LEARNING THE SKILLS

As stated at the beginning of this chapter, theological assessment is the art of thinking theologically about the beliefs that undergird parishioners' feelings and actions. It involves identifying the theological category(s) (guilt, anxiety, and anger) and the subcategories (acceptance-despair, hope-dread, and love-alienation) that fit parishioners' central feelings and related beliefs (see Table 1). Theological assessment gives pastors guidance in determining the arguments and religious resources they can use in stages 2 and 3 to dispute unhelpful beliefs and affirm gospel ones (see Table 2).

TABLE 1

Category	*Anxiety*		*Guilt*		*Anger*	
Subcategories	Hope	Dread	Acceptance	Despair	Love	Alienation

Theological disputation is the process of teaching the good news and challenging nongospel beliefs. This chapter has provided both rational and theological arguments to be used in exposing the weakness of the beliefs that lie behind despair, dread, and alienation. It has also given scriptural support for those ideas that promote acceptance, hope, and love.

TABLE 2

Subcategories/Ideas

Dread	*Despair*	*Alienation*
Anxious overconcern	Demand for approval	Condemning the offender
Problem avoidance	High self-expectations	Low frustration tolerance
Passive happiness	Condemning the offender	Need for perfection

Theological assessment and disputation are the pastoral skills through which pastors offer their unique contribution to care—theological perspective.

Process

The process of learning theological assessment and disputation requires patience with oneself because it is the most complex pair of skills presented in this book. Theological assessment requires that the pastor: (1) place the parishioner's major feeling and belief in one of the major categories (guilt, anxiety, and anger) and the appropriate subcategory (despair or acceptance, dread or hope, alienation or love); (2) decide which beliefs to challenge; and (3) choose the argument to use. Theological disputation involves picking the strategy for presenting that argument and then actually challenging the parishioner's belief(s).

As with the other skills, learning theological assessment and disputation requires practice. The particular form of training that is most effective is the regular theological assessment and disputation of your own issues because it gives you a personal knowledge of the procedure and its benefits. Frequent practice in theological assessment of other's issues is also necessary to acquaint you with other's styles of thinking; this is best done in a practice group. After you use these two methods for a while, you will find that you have gained an intuitive grasp on the method that allows you to do theological assessment almost automatically.

Exercises

These exercises build on the assessments of others and yourself that are the results of doing the exercises "Practicing the Presence Skills" (4A and 4B) at the end of chapter 3.

1. *Practicing theological assessment and disputation on your issues*

   Review the written pastoral conversation that you did for exercise 4A. Identify the dominant feelings and beliefs that undergird them. Place your core perspective in one of the three assessment categories and one of its subcategories and write this down. For instance, Martha's core perspective would fall in the category of anxiety and the subcategory of dread.

   After doing the assessment, read the arguments that challenge your belief if it is unhelpful or support it if it is helpful. Choose the argument that is most persuasive for you and write it on the same paper as the assessment. Rehearse this argument every time the issue comes up for you. Finally, write down your reflections on doing this exercise.

2. *Preparing theological assessment and disputation for practice*

   Preparation: Reflect on the presence skill conversation you did in exercise 4B. Put the feelings and beliefs you assessed in a theological assessment category and subcategory. Memorize the arguments in this chapter that could be used in challenging or affirming one of their beliefs. Pick additional Scripture verses or arguments that could be used.

5

Proclamation

IN STAGE 2 PARISHIONERS HAVE TWO TASKS: first, to understand that their perspectives contribute to their problems or joys; and second, to understand the freeing perspective of the gospel. Pastors enable parishioners' understanding by *proclamation*. Pastors' proclamations are based on their theological assessments of the beliefs that undergird parishioners' problems or joyful feelings and behaviors. Once these beliefs have been identified, they can be disputed or affirmed using the proclamation skills.

There are five proclamation skills: informing, sharing, confronting, contending, and reviewing. *Informing* is communicating needed information and correcting harmful misinformation. *Sharing* consists of offering a portion of pastors' experiences to parishioners. Inviting parishioners to examine the differences between their perceptions and pastors' defines *confronting*. *Contending* involves disputing parishioners' irrational beliefs by using reason and religious resources. Inviting parishioners to summarize their understanding is the concluding skill of *reviewing*.

Using the proclamation skills is more difficult than using the presence skills because pastors have to choose from among the proclamation skills, whereas almost all of the presence skills are used in stage 1 and beyond. Because the Holy Spirit speaks directly to the parishioners, quite often the best challenge is one that draws out the challenges that the Spirit is already making within them. Thus probes that lead to self-challenges are frequently the best form of proclamation. Next in line are the milder proclamation skills of informing and sharing; then follow the milder forms of confronting and contending. Last, because they are least evocative of self-challenge, but often useful when milder forms have not worked, are direct confronting and direct contending.

Because the Holy Spirit speaks directly to parishioners it is usually not necessary to share all of the arguments and Scripture verses from the theological assessment chapter in proclamation. These disputations are used as a framework to help you identify the Spirit's disputations of irrational ideas and affirmations of gospel beliefs that are already in parishioners' stories. It is these disputations and affirmations that you point to, draw out, and affirm when you use the proclamation skills.

The following verbatim illustrates the skills and process of proclamation.

THE PAIN OF DEATH

This conversation is between Doris Thomas, who supervises the lay visitor program, and Sam Peters, a visitor. They are having a second discussion about Sam's difficulty with visiting James, a bedridden parishioner who is dying and cannot speak. In the previous conversation Doris had helped Sam to begin to face the idea that James, who is about the same age as Sam, arouses his fear of death. In the first part of this conversation Doris helped Sam acknowledge that part of him wants to visit James and part does not—and that the part that does not is blocked by fear. The conversation is divided into two sections: It begins with stage 1, assessing, and continues with the stage 2 step of proclaiming.

Assessing

DORIS: OK, let me see if I understand where you are. Part of you wants to visit James and part is scared to death of facing him. So what you would like to come out of this conversation is somehow for the part of you that is scared to death and very uncomfortable to . . . ah . . . be free to cooperate and go visit.

SAM: That's right!

DORIS: You visit him twice a month; what has been successful in getting that part of you to go along?

SAM: The reason that I still go is because I suppose . . . I haven't really thought about it too much . . . [Doris says, "OK."] . . . But, I guess the reason that I still go is that I feel a duty [*emphasized*] to go. [Doris says, "Uh-huh."] That I feel like I want to be true to my responsibilities as a visitor. I want to . . . I want to be a good visitor.

DORIS: Uh-huh. So the thing that has been most helpful in getting the frightened part to go is your sense of duty.

SAM: Ah . . . Yes, I would say that.

DORIS: And that has been fairly successful in the sense that it has worked twice a month.

SAM: Uh-huh. Also there is another part of that in that I can say that I love the man. [Doris says, "Uh-huh."] I do feel a kinship with him. [Doris says, "Uh-huh."] And I think I feel more of a kinship with him now than in the beginning. So we have developed a relationship over the past few months, even though he can't express that relationship to me I still feel that we have a relationship.

DORIS: OK, so the second thing is that you developed some relationship by going out of duty. [Sam says, "Uh-huh."] So you have two things that are helping you go.

SAM: Uh-huh. But then also the relationship part of it . . . it would be easier if I didn't go because then I could start the grief process because I know that he's going to die sometime very soon.

DORIS: Uh-huh. So the relationship itself is a little painful. I have a hunch that's because he can't respond, and you see death coming up on the horizon.

Sam: I think your hunch is accurate. . . . I would say your hunch is accurate.

DORIS: On the one hand you are saying that you are visiting him twice a month, and yet on the other hand you are asking for something to help you to get you to visit him? I'm confused.

SAM: I want help to visit him, painlessly!

DORIS: Oh. So the thing that's going on is that you are looking for a painless way to visit him.

SAM: I don't like pain! [*Interjected emphatically*]

DORIS: Uh-huh . . . it seems to me, as I am thinking about it, and please test it out—what you want is to visit the person without pain because the lack of pain would indicate that you were doing it right and you really want to do things just right.

SAM: That's right, that's exactly it.

DORIS: What's right?

SAM: What you said, that I want to do things the right way and I know that this can't be the right way because it hurts so much.

Proclaiming

DORIS: Ah . . . and I am wondering whether another way to look at this would be for you to accept that the painful part of doing it is in fact accepting the ministry. Accepting the pain is part of it. It is not an indication of something wrong with it or you. Jesus in the Garden of Gethsemane does not seem to want to accept the cup, he just accepts it.

SAM: Hmm. [*Long pause*] I am trying to put this in my own way of thinking. [Doris says, "Uh-huh."] And I know that you are right. He accepted it in one sense willingly. [Doris says, "Uh-huh."] He did it freely of his own volition. But in another sense it would have been a lot easier and a lot less painful if that cup could have been taken from him.

DORIS: And a lot less inspiring. It probably wouldn't have made the Bible. [*Said with a smile*]

SAM: [*Long pause*] You want to say something? I don't know what you mean.

DORIS: What I mean is that if what Jesus did had not been painful then it would not have been inspiring for us. It would not have made the New Testament pages. On the other hand, if Jesus had run to the cross joyously and excitedly, he would have just been pronounced insane—he wouldn't have been crucified. I am saying that carrying the pain—willingly accepting the pain, yet not loving it—is the essence of ministry.

SAM: So . . . possibly . . . what I am doing is more in terms of examining my own call—whether or not I am willing to follow it.

DORIS: No, I guess that wasn't what I was saying. What I was trying to say was that . . . ah . . . You have decided that what you are doing, visiting James while feeling the pain, is wrong. I disagree. I believe that your *idea* that you're not supposed to feel pain is the problem [Sam says, "Uh-huh."] not the bad feeling. The bad feeling is normal, healthy, and necessary in ministry. The idea that you're not supposed to feel bad intensifies your discomfort. That *idea* makes you anxious about what you are doing. Does that make sense to you?

SAM: So what you are saying is that feeling pain about what I am doing is all right because Jesus experienced pain doing his ministry, but my real problem is my idea that I'm not supposed to feel this way.

DORIS: That's right.

SAM: I'm confused about how the idea is my real problem.

DORIS: Do you remember what I have said last week about the situation not causing the disabling feelings, that our thoughts about the situation do. [Sam says, "Uh-huh."] Well, I believe that is what is happening in this situation. Your discomfort with watching James die is upsetting but it's not what is causing you to be so anxious that you even question your vocation as a visitor. What's causing that is your idea that you are not supposed to feel pain when visiting him because feeling that way proves you are not a good visitor—that idea makes you so anxious.

SAM: You mean that the voice that keeps telling me that a good visitor isn't as scared as I am is the thing that is upsetting me.

DORIS: Yep . . . ah . . . I know that voice well—it upsets me, too.

SAM: You hear it too, but you are so good at this.

DORIS: Being good has nothing to do with it, that voice upsets a lot of us.

SAM: I'm glad that I'm not the only one. [*Pause*] This has been real helpful.

DORIS: How has it been helpful?

SAM: Well . . . I feel better about myself because I'm not the only one that experiences pain when I try to minister . . . and . . . the thing about my ideas making the problem worse . . . both were helpful. What I want to know now is how do I deal with this voice I keep hearing?

Analysis

This is a verbatim of a stage 2 conversation in which the pastor helps the parishioner acknowledge his part in the problem with visiting a dying parishioner and accept the good news that the troubles he has are part of ministry.

Assessing. The transcript begins with a summary that pulls together the earlier parts of the conversation and lays a foundation for assessment. Doris continues assessing by challenging Sam with a probe designed to get him to acknowledge his strengths, and then she goes on to examine Sam's responses to this challenge through paraphrases, probes, and a hunch. After exploring his strengths and finding them adequate to the task, Doris confronts him again to get at the reason that Sam thinks he has a problem even though he is carrying out the task adequately. After first examining Sam's response to the challenge with a paraphrase, Doris continues the examination with a hunch that uncovers the irrational belief behind the anxiety—need for perfection (cf. anxiety in chapter 4). Sam confirms this hunch. Doris then probes for two reasons: first to determine what he is affirming, and second to get him to reinforce this assessment by stating it again in his own words.

Proclaiming. Doris disputes the irrational belief. She instructs Sam using a combination of information giving (the new perspective) and contending (the example from the Gospels). In response to Sam's statement, Doris contends using humor by saying that if Jesus had not felt pain, it wouldn't be in the Bible, but it escapes Sam. Doris explains herself and continues her contending and Sam misses the point again. She then tries information giving, and Sam finally understands. Sam's difficulty with understanding Doris is to be noted as it is a clue that the material being discussed is emotionally important enough to raise his defenses and constrict his awareness of humor.

Sam's question about how an idea can be the problem indicates to Doris that he has not related this conversation to her presentations on the metanoia model, so she summarizes the basic theory briefly—an example of information giving. After Sam shows that he understands, the pastor proclaims the good news that Sam is not alone in having this problem by sharing and informing.

Review. When Sam indicates that he has accepted some of the good news Doris helps him to celebrate and reinforce this understanding by a probe. After Sam successfully summarizes his understanding, he issues an invitation to move to stage 3, "What I want to know now is how do I deal with this voice I keep hearing?"

FACILITATIVE CONDITIONS

Gaining a new understanding (the goal of stage 2) is difficult for parishioners because their irrational beliefs are deeply held, emotionally powerful habits of thinking that are resistant to change. Pastors can minimize this resistance by making sure that their challenges express the four facilitative conditions that researchers have established as essential for an effective helping relationship: empathy, respect, genuineness, and concreteness (Rogers, 1961; Carkhuff, 1969; Gurman and Razin, 1977).

Empathy

Empathy, understanding things from parishioners' points of view, has been discussed in chapters 1, 2, and 3 and is the goal of the presence skills. Empathy is important in stage 2 in two ways: first, proclamations are based on it; and second, the presence skills are used after each proclamation to learn about parishioners' understanding of the pastor's challenges. My image for this process is the waltz—*one*-two-three, *one*-two-three. The one represents the proclamation statement and the two and three represent the several responding statements that enable parishioners to explore their responses to that challenge. For example, in the preceding verbatim, Doris uses two probes, a paraphrase, and a hunch in order to understand Sam's response to her query about how Sam has been successful in visiting James.

Respect

Positive regard or nonpossessive warmth for parishioners is *respect* for them. Challenges that are not judgmental and invite the parishioners' responses are respectful. Doris challenges Sam respectfully about the fact that he is already visiting James twice a month by laying out the conflicting evidence and stating that she is confused. She thus invites his response. A less respectful challenge would have simply accused Sam of saying opposite things that do not make sense—handing him a conclusion instead of a problem and thus inviting a defense instead of a dialogue.

Genuineness

Congruence between pastors' expressions and their feelings is *genuineness*. This authenticity involves relating to parishioners without either defensiveness or retreating into roles. Appropriate self-disclosure as a part of proclamation both models and inspires the authenticity that comes from letting go of the musts. Doris illustrates this by briefly sharing that she hears "the voice," too, directing her statement toward challenging Sam's guilt. Another expression of genuineness is the willingness to risk and persist in sharing one's opinions. Doris patiently offers her insight, in spite of Sam's difficulty in understanding it.

Concreteness

The fourth facilitative condition is *concreteness*—specificity of expression. Challenges are more effective if they are directly related to parishioners' statements instead of abstract generalizations. Doris confuses Sam by her statement, "And a lot less inspiring. It probably wouldn't have made the Bible," because she does not carefully link her insight to Sam's preceding statement; it is not concrete. She tries to make up for this, in her next two comments, which are very specific—speaking about last week, Sam's discomfort with James, and the idea about what causes upset. Sam then understands this complex idea.

The four facilitative conditions each and in combination strengthen pastors' relationships with parishioners. A strong pastoral relationship helps people deal with their resistance to be challenged.

INFORMING

Informing is communicating needed information and correcting harmful misinformation. Giving information in a pastoral conversation is different from lecturing in a classroom in three key ways: (1) it is briefer, (2) it is focused on one specific belief, (3) it is in response to a parishioner's immediate need. Pastors use informing for three purposes—to change an unhelpful belief, to support a helpful belief, and to provide a new perspective.

Because conveying values and teaching beliefs is central to the pastoral role, they are part of the information that pastors give. Therefore informing will often consist of instructing people about the gospel beliefs. Nonreligious counselors, on the other hand, are not supposed to impose their values and beliefs.

Feeling Harried

For example, Jan is a thirty-six-year-old who has recently returned to work after having her first child. The baby is now four months old. Jan works as a supervisor of ten employees in a "people-intensive" job. Her husband is highly involved in his job, which requires him to work long hours and some weekends, as well as travel at least once a month. Jan is talking to Jill, who helped prepare her, Kathy, and Sue for adult baptism three years ago.

JAN: Plenty of other women have no trouble taking care of a baby and working. What's wrong with me?

JILL: You feel incompetent because you are having difficulty returning to work and continuing to do most of the child care.

JAN: Yeah, everybody else seems to be doing fine with both. I saw Kathy and Sue at church last Sunday and they didn't look nearly as harried as I felt.

JILL: It seems to me that you are guilty because you believe that you should be more competent than you are.

JAN: Well, I *should* be able to handle it as well as others.

JILL: Did you know that Kathy, Sue, and some other women felt pretty much like you do, so they formed a support group to help them weather the storm?

JAN: No! I thought I was the only one having troubles.

JILL: You know, I've learned that the idea that I should be able to handle everything competently or I'm worthless is what keeps me and many others feeling that there's something wrong with us.

JAN: You mean like I'm doing about the baby and work.

JILL: Uh-huh. [*Nodding head up and down*]

JAN: It's the idea that I'm supposed to be able to handle it that's making me feel so bad? I don't understand.

JILL: Well, the way I learned it is that "It's not the situation that makes us feel bad, it's our beliefs about the situation that make us feel bad." Therefore, if you want to feel better you need to change your beliefs. [*The conversation continues*]

Analysis

In this example Jill prepares for proclamation by assessing, "It seems to me that you feel guilty because you believe that you should be more competent than you are." Then she uses the skill of informing. Notice that her statements are brief and in direct response to Jan's needs. Even though information giving does not have to be this brief, conciseness is the desired direction for this skill. Jill's informing challenges Jan's unhelpful belief (high self-expectations). The verbatim ends with Jill trying to enlarge Jan's perspective by introducing the theory behind the metanoia model.

In this example Jill conveys the good news of God's acceptance by informing Jan that others are not meeting the standards by which she is judging herself, and that's all right. Jill could have informed Jan more directly of the gospel by teaching her that we are justified by grace and not by works. Thus informing can be done with information that either indirectly (as in the example) or directly (as suggested here) communicates God's acceptance, power, and love.

SHARING

Sharing is offering a portion of pastors' experiences to parishioners. It is a form of proclamation that challenges parishioners in two ways. First, it challenges them to disclose their feelings and related beliefs by giving an example that both shows them how it is done and encourages them to do it. This modeling is important because many parishioners need guidance in either expressing their feelings or acknowledging the part that their beliefs play in them. Second, sharing is a way of challenging the beliefs that their problems are peculiar to them and that such problems cannot be managed. Pastors challenge these beliefs by sharing their struggles with similar issues.

Sharing can be effective if several cautions are observed:
- It is not a form of bragging about how good or disciplined the pastor is. It is, rather, a way of testifying to God's presence, love, and power with thankfulness and awe.

- It is to be used infrequently, so that it gives the parishioners a model but does not change the discussion from their issues to pastors' issues. Frequent self-sharing is an indication that pastors are working on their own issues in the conversation.
- It is to be brief and focused on parishioners' issues. Long, unfocused sharing draws parishioners' attention away from their own issues and to their pastors' issues.

Worried about the Wedding

For example, Joe and Rebecca are preparing to marry. As part of the marriage preparation each meets for a discussion with the same-gender member of a lay couple. Rudy is the layperson who is acting as pastor to Joe in this conversation. The example begins midway through the conversation.

JOE: You know, Rudy, I don't know how to say it, but I have some questions.

RUDY: Questions?

JOE: Yeah, about this whole thing. I just don't know if Becca's ready for all this marriage business. She's kind of young and wild—not totally flaky—but kind of, you know . . . independent . . . you know what I mean?

RUDY: You're a little concerned about marrying her because you worry if she's ready.

JOE: That's right. And . . . when I really think about it sometimes, I kind of wonder if . . . you know . . . I'm ready [*Said with voice trailing off*] . . . I mean if I were ready I wouldn't be feeling tense now, would I?

RUDY: You are worried about your readiness because you are a bit uptight about getting married.

JOE: Yeah, I'm glad you understand because if the truth be known, I am more than a little bit uptight about it. I have been having a hard time concentrating at work, probably because I am waking up in the middle of the night and not getting back to sleep. That's a sign that I'm not ready, isn't it?

RUDY: Let me get this straight. You find yourself so tense about the marriage that you are wondering whether your being upset is an indication that you are not ready to get married. And you want to know if I agree that this is a sign?

JOE: That's right, the pastor said that you knew a lot about those kind of things.

RUDY: Well, I don't know what you need to do in your situation but I can tell you that the month before Rose and I got married I was in such bad shape that I couldn't sleep, or work either. I was a mess. I guess the worst thing that happened was when I went to sleep while driving my dad's tractor and rammed it into a tree. I guess God takes care of babes and fools, because nothing got hurt but my pride.

JOE: That happened to you, even though you were marrying someone as nice and stable as your wife is?

RUDY: Yep. You must remember that Rose wasn't always as settled as she is now. But, more important, I was more worried about me than I was about her.

JOE: Well you don't know how good it makes me feel that you had some of the same kind of tenseness before you got married that I have. [*The conversation continues*]

Analysis

After carefully assessing, in the first part of this excerpt, Rudy then uses the skill of sharing. Notice that the bit of experience shared is the opposite of bragging. Rather, it shows that the pastor also had difficulty handling the situation and it witnesses to God's power to sustain. Notice, also, that the story was compressed so as to speak to the point without distracting the parishioner. The two purposes of this sharing were to let the parishioner know that his situation was not unique and to confirm his insight that it was not the bride's readiness that was making him anxious.

CONFRONTATION

Confronting is inviting parishioners to examine the differences between their perceptions and pastors' perceptions.

Some common differences in perception are:
- A large discrepancy between what they say and what they do. Example: Bill says he wants to learn more about the Bible, but he frequently misses class and when he comes he is unprepared.
- A significant difference between the way they see themselves and the ways others see them. Example: George sees himself as smart; his teachers see him as average at best.
- A contrast between the things they say and the way they feel. Example: Mary says that she is feeling fine, but her facial expression and her tone of voice indicate that she may be in pain.

• The way they see the situation and the way others see it. Example: Lois sees her son as out to embarrass her; her pastor sees his behavior as that of a normal teenager.

Confronting focuses on different perceptions of the way parishioners Feel, Experience, Act or Think (FEAT). When parishioners and pastors have these differences, pastors help them by confronting their perceptions.

Because it challenges parishioners' perceptions more directly, confronting is stronger medicine than informing and sharing. Thus, confronting is more likely to raise parishioners' resistances than those other challenges. Pastors often play into parishioners' resistances by attacking their perceptions in an attempt "to set parishioners straight" or "get something off our chests" rather than employing the facilitative conditions (empathy, concreteness, genuineness, and respect) in confronting parishioners' perceptions.

Two Formulas

Carkhuff has developed two formulas for facilitative confronting—one for mild confrontations and another for direct confrontations (1979, 116–19). The first formula is: "On the one hand, you [feel, experience, act, or think _____], and, on the other hand, you [FEAT _____]." This formula invites parishioners to reconcile the discrepancy. Thus they are challenged to either show how the two fit together or to admit that they do not fit. Mild confrontation is done "in terms that come entirely from the helpee's [parishioner's] own frame of reference."

For example, Sue Smith is the senior pastor of a church. The parishioner is George Johnson, an active member of the congregation. They have been talking about George's drinking habits. Sue says, "On the one hand you tell me that you go to a bar and drink 'three or four beers' between five and six every afternoon and on the other hand you tell me that you 'do not drink much.' " The words in quotation marks are direct quotes from the parishioner.

The following formula is for direct confrontation: You say that you [feel, experience, act, think] _____ but it looks to me like you [FEAT _____]. The direct confrontation is based on data that the pastor can observe independently. Skilled pastors will only use direct confrontation when two conditions are met: they have enough data to back up their statements and when other challenging skills, including mild confrontation, have not helped.

In the example here, George responds to Sue, "You don't understand, pastor—drinking beers is not really drinking. It's not drinking unless you are into the hard stuff. A few beers don't bother me. 'It's just a pause that refreshes' that I take before I go home." Sue answers, "You say it doesn't bother you but there seems to be a pattern of things that happen after the 5 P.M. to 6 P.M. beer-drinking period that indicates heavy drinking. For instance: the finance committee chair says that you were acting tipsy at the last two 7 P.M. meetings; your wife says that you fell asleep or got into an argument with the children immediately after you got home at 6:30 three of the last six days; and the police tell me that you were arrested for drunk driving yesterday at 6:15 P.M."

Nonfacilitative Confrontation

If Sue had withheld her perspective completely or hidden it in a question she would not have been communicating genuineness. Sue could have responded to George in several nonfacilitative ways. For example, she could have said, "Well, I hope you know what you are doing," or "Don't you think three or four beers is a lot in an hour?" A common way to show disrespect is to attack the character of the person instead of confronting him or her with the data. For example, Sue could have scolded George, saying, "Why do you sit there and tell me the nonsense that three or four beers is not drinking? You must think that I am stupid."

None of these responses to George's statement would be facilitative.

CONTENDING

Contending is disputing parishioners' idolatrous beliefs by using reason and religious resources. Contending is a form of challenging that contrasts parishioners' self-defeating ideas with the clarifying perspective of reason or the liberating perspective of the gospel, or both. Thus, contending with religious resources is different from informing in that it is a more direct challenge to parishioners' beliefs.\ It differs from confronting in that contending disputes beliefs whereas confronting states differences between descriptions of behaviors.\ There are summaries of rational and gospel arguments that can be used in contending in chapter 4 under the three theological assessment categories: guilt, anxiety, and anger.

Reasoning

One strategy for contending with irrational beliefs is *reasoning*. The parishioner can be shown that these ideas do not make sense, are not effective, or do not jibe with either the parishioner's or the community's experience. A key question for the parishioner to answer is, "What is the evidence for this belief? Logic alone is usually not sufficient to dispute unhelpful ideas. Parishioners' emotions must be involved also. Emotionally involving methods of presenting arguments are inviting self-challenge, humor, facing the worst, and affirming beliefs.

Inviting self-challenge.   Self-challenge is usually more convincing than challenges by others; thus, it is a preferred way to contend. Self-challenge can be invited by such probes as: How is it (the belief) working for you? Are the things you're telling yourself about this experience helping you? What else could you tell yourself?

For example, Jerry, who is having difficulty carrying out his committee responsibilities, is talking with Betsy, the committee chair. Jerry says, "I keep thinking if I don't do it right, I shouldn't do it at all." Betsy replies, "How is that belief working for you?" Jerry answers, "It's tying me up; it's tough to get started." By asking a question, Betsy gets Jerry to confront himself with the effect that his irrational idea is having on his performance as a committee member.

Humor.   Humor puts things in perspective and relieves tension. Humor can be a deathblow to the out-of-perspective tension caused by irrational beliefs. Greiger and Boyd (1980, 153) put it this way: "Human emotional disturbance largely consists of people taking themselves, others, and life events too seriously."

The trick is to make fun of the ideas and not the parishioners. Thus it must be done respectfully in the context of a strong pastoral relationship. One way to communicate this respect is to identify with parishioners who hold this idea by sharing.

To continue with the example of the conversation between Betsy and Jerry, after Jerry's response has been explored, Betsy says, "I know what you mean. Sometimes when I try to push down on the accelerator, I end up with one foot in my mouth and the other on the brakes." Betsy identifies with Jerry by sharing her feelings about a similar problem, and she tries to break the tension by using a ridiculous image. It must be remembered, however, that sometimes humor does not work, either because the comment is not funny or the parishioners are too wound up to get the joke. Further, what is humorous to one person or in one situation is not to another person or in a different situation.

Facing the worst. One way to defuse parishioners' terror about the consequences of their actions is to help them *face the worst* case. Discussing the unmentionable horror begins to make it less terrifying. The frightening possibility can be domesticated further by discussing alternative ways to respond to the feared consequences.

Continuing with the example, after exploring Jerry's response to her humorous statement, Betsy invites him to face the worst. She asks, "What is the worst thing that could happen if you gave a poor report?" Jerry replies, "It would be a sacrilege, like not taking God's work seriously." Betsy asks, "And what do you think God would do to you for committing such a sacrilege?" Jerry answers, "I don't know . . . it just wouldn't be right. I guess it wouldn't be the end of the world." Betsy probes to get Jerry to face the worst. Once he states his horror at the possibility of a poor report, it begins to defuse.

Affirming beliefs. The process of *affirming beliefs* consists of celebrating parishioners' helpful beliefs. By strengthening helpful beliefs pastors dilute the power of unhelpful beliefs. Affirming is a positive way to contend with negative ideas; it crowds them out.

The example, the conversation between Betsy and Jerry, continues. Betsy says, "It wouldn't be the end of the world?" Jerry says, "No, of course it wouldn't. It's not like the church would fall down, or millions would starve or anything like that." Betsy asks, "Turning in a poor report is not that earth-shattering?" By probing, Betsy helps Jerry explore, and thus celebrate or reinforce, his insight that turning in a poor report is not a total catastrophe.

When reason is used to contend with parishioners' unhelpful beliefs, it should be emotionally involving and related to parishioners' experiences. Inviting self-challenge, using humor, having people face the worst, and affirming beliefs are four techniques that meet those criteria.

Religious Resources

A second and powerful tactic is contending using religious resources, because they stir many parishioners to their deeps. Resources such as prayer, Scripture, and the rites have the power to bring up the subconscious feelings, experiences, and thoughts that lie behind irrational beliefs. These can be explored when they become conscious. A second contribution that religious resources make is that they instruct parishioners in helpful or gospel beliefs. This instruction is strengthened by familiarity and repetition when resources chosen, such as commonly used prayers and Scripture verses, are familiar.

Two formats.   The pastor may use a format for contrasting parishioners' idolatrous beliefs with religious resources that is similar to that of a mild confrontation. Your idea is _____; (the resource—Scripture, etc.) says _____. How do you fit the two together? The importance of this format is that it invites parishioners to challenge themselves.

For example, a pastor may say to a parishioner, "You say that 'what he did was unforgivable,' yet we pray, 'Forgive us our sins as we forgive those who sin against us.' How have you dealt with that?" A more direct form is: You think this but from (the resources) it is clear that _____ . As in the case with direct confrontation, this second form is to be used if the first is not effective.

In this example, the parishioner replies, "I am sure that the Lord doesn't expect me to forgive a louse like that. What he did was beneath contempt. He betrayed his child . . . and he betrayed me. He doesn't deserve to be forgiven. No one should get away with taking advantage of the defenseless . . . I don't care who it is."

The pastor responds, "I agree that what he did was awful, but the fact is your lack of forgiveness is punishing you—not him. You are the one who is 'all tied up in knots,' 'unable to concentrate at work,' and 'uncomfortable around your old friends' because you're carrying this load of anger. Part of the truth of 'forgive us our sins as we forgive the sins of others' is that we are not released from our painful angers until we forgive the other. Does that ring true?"

Reflection on the formats.   In the first example the pastor uses a religious resource, the Lord's Prayer, which is well known and highly valued by the parishioner. The Lord's Prayer is a resource that is used frequently. In the second example, the pastor uses the parishioner's own experience to give more emotional power to the disputation. The pastor also explains the reason for forgiveness in language that will make sense to the parishioner.

Reason and religious resources are two good methods for fighting idolatrous beliefs. Their power is multiplied when they are used skillfully together. There are no methods or combinations, however, that will eliminate all resistance.

REVIEWING

Reviewing is the skill of inviting parishioners to summarize their understanding of pastors' proclamations. It is used at the conclusion of stage 2 to help parishioners clarify and solidify the insights they have gained in understanding both how their perspectives contribute to their problem or joy and how the gospel relates to their beliefs. By inviting parishioners to review their grasp of the pastor's proclamation, the pastor has a chance to correct or fill out any inadequacies in understanding.

The process of reviewing is simple. Pastors use a probe to invite parishioners to offer a summary. What insight have you gained? How would you summarize what we have said? are the types of questions that invite a review.

The reviewing that concludes stage 2 is the reverse of the summarizing that ends stage 1. In stage 1 (exploring) the emphasis is on what parishioners say, so pastors summarize to help themselves understand. In stage 2 (understanding) there is more focus on pastors' perspectives. Therefore, parishioners review (summarize) in order to understand.

PROCLAMATION, CONDEMNATION, AND ABDICATION

Proclamation is difficult. It involves challenging parishioners' perspectives while communicating respect by inviting dialogue and avoiding being judgmental. On the one hand, pastors must express their own feelings and thoughts (genuineness), yet on the other they must continue being empathic with parishioners. Finally, pastors are to make their challenges concrete, not abstract. Because the task of proclamation is so difficult, pastors often drift from it into simpler alternatives—condemnation and abdication. This section presents the differences in style between these three responses to the task of challenging parishioners' perspectives.

Proclamation

Proclamation is characterized by an assertive style of communication. Being assertive means offering reflections in a serious but tentative manner. Seriousness is shown by two key behaviors: sharing thoughts in clear, direct, succinct, and concrete statements, and steadfastly continuing to share that point until it is heard (but not necessarily agreed with) rather than bouncing from idea to idea. Tentativeness is manifested when pastors acknowledge their incomplete knowledge and invite parishioners' responses.

The following statement by a pastor is an example of proclamation: "When you described your teacher, your voice was high-pitched, you spoke rapidly, you frowned, and clenched your fist. It seemed to me that you were angry at the teacher. Is that the way you would talk about your feelings?" Notice that the pastor ends with phrases that acknowledge limited understanding and ask for the parishioner's reaction: "It seemed to me . . ." and "Is that the way you would talk about your feelings?" The dialogical style of proclamation communicates pastors' genuineness and respect for parishioners. Proclamation is loving communication.

Condemnation

Condemnation is distinguished by an aggressive way of presenting understandings. The strength of this style is the seriousness with which the perspective is offered; its weakness is a lack of tentativeness, concreteness, succinctness or some combination of the three. Parishioners experience verbose, abstract, and nontentative monologues as judgmental, whether or not they are intended to be. In the situation described in the preceding paragraph, a condemning pastor might say, "The feelings that you have in this situation are not helpful—they show all over, you know. They will get you nowhere. You have to learn how to get along with people, you know. I don't mean to come down too hard on you, but I hope you can see what I am talking about—because it is important that you deal with this situation before it gets out of hand. I know because I have seen similar situations get out of hand before—all because these kinds of feelings were not dealt with at once. Let me suggest some ways that you can deal with this. . . ." The pastor continues with a plan. Though this pastor states that he has no intention to condemn ("I don't mean to come down too hard on you"), the abstractness, length, and monological style of this response combine to convey a lack of respect for the parishioner. Condemnation is alienated communication.

Abdication

By contrast, *abdication* is set apart by a passive mode of presenting pastors' opinions. Abdicators seek to distance themselves from the aggressive style of the condemners by emphasizing tentativeness, often to the extreme of refusing to state their thoughts. In the process they deprive parishioners of the opportunity to examine their perspectives. Abdication can be identified by one or more of the following patterns: long apologies for one's opinion or for offering it, bouncing from observation to observation without pursuing any point in depth, not offering any challenge at all. For example, an abdicating pastor might respond to the situation described in the previous paragraphs in several ways. The pastor might say, "I do not know whether I am right or not and I hope you excuse me for saying this—I don't mean to be harsh, but I was wondering if you might be having some feelings about your teacher? I don't know, what do you think?" The pastor might say briefly, "I 'sorta' think that you and the teacher have something going on." The parishioner replies, "We are getting along all right." The pastor then says, "Well, I guess I missed it. I was interested in what you said about having too much homework. Do you think that was the problem?" Or the pastor might simply summarize, saying, "Your teacher calls on others more than you, and assigns a lot of homework."

Whereas condemnation features a monologue by the pastor, abdication encourages one by the parishioner. Because abdicating pastors do not model genuineness in communication, they have difficulty helping parishioners engage in constructive self-disclosure. Like its reverse, condemnation, abdication is alienated communication.

Three Styles Compared

The three styles of challenging are summarized in Table 1 below.

TABLE 1
A Comparison of Challenging Styles

CONDEMNATION	PROCLAMATION	ABDICATION
Aggressive	*Assertive*	*Passive*
Judgmental	Respectful	Nonjudgmental
Imposing	Sharing	Abdicating
Not Empathic	Empathic	Not Empathic
Abstract	Concrete	Abstract
Monologue (pastor)	Dialogue	Monologue (parishioner)

When pastors drift into condemnation and abdication, it is often an indication that they have unresolved guilt, anxiety, or anger about one or more of the following: the parishioner, the subject of the conversation, or the dynamics of the conversation. It is important that we pay attention to our FEAT as we challenge parishioners. Fortunately, we do not have to be perfectly resolved on all issues in order to do proclamation well; it is important, however, that we are in the process of resolving our guilt, anxiety, or anger in some area of our lives, so that we can communicate the freedom, power, and joy that this process brings. These experiences motivate us to use the proclamation style to invite parishioners to share in the joy that we have known.

LEARNING THE SKILLS

Pastors use the proclamation skills to share their perspectives with parishioners in a way that helps the latter to understand their problem or joy better. Four of the proclamation skills—informing, sharing, confronting, and contending—are designed to challenge parishioners first to understand the role of their beliefs in creating their feelings and behaviors, and second to accept the gospel beliefs. The fifth skill, reviewing, aids parishioners in remembering the insights they gain from the conversation. Assessing, or identifying parishioners' beliefs, is the presence skill that prepares for the proclamation skills that challenge unhelpful and affirm helpful beliefs.

In order to make their challenges more effective, pastors style them to incorporate the facilitative conditions. Skillful proclamation is assertive love because it is based on empathy and embodies respect, genuineness, and concreteness. By contrast, nonfacilitative challenges express alienation in either its passive or aggressive forms.

Process

Doing the proclamation skills feels awkward to most pastors at first. Those who are comfortable with a nondirective style are uncomfortable challenging parishioners' beliefs. Similarly, those who are more directive have difficulty with the limitations that the skills put on their directiveness. Pastors who are used to integrating Scripture or theological terms into their conversation have difficulty understanding many types of informing, sharing, and confronting as proclamation. Likewise, those who are uneasy about scriptural or theological vocabulary have trouble with using it in their contending. Almost everyone has trouble deciding when to use which skill.

Like all of the other skills, comfort with the proclamation skills increases with practice. The ability to integrate the scriptural and theological vocabulary naturally into proclamation grows with practice in using theological assessment and disputation on pastors' own issues and beliefs. Acceptance of informing, sharing, and confronting as proclaiming the good news, even when they do not use religious language, develops as one rehearses thinking of the Holy Spirit speaking directly to parishioners in their own language and experiences. Remember that most of the special scriptural language that we now set apart was once the normal everyday language of the people.

In sum, proclamation is much less straightforward than presence. It is a greater challenge to pastors' creativity. Proclamation is more uniquely pastoral than presence because it involves theological assessment and religious resources—two key pastoral tools.

Exercises

1. Preparing to Proclaim

Informing: Summarize a person's problem, noting the irrational belief that is part of it. Decide what information is needed to correct this belief. Write a statement in the form that you would share with the person. Evaluate your statement by the standards given in chapter 5.

Sharing: Summarize a person's problem, noting the irrational belief that is part of it. Recall a situation in which you struggled with that or a similar belief. Write a statement in the form you would share with the person who has the problem. Evaluate your statement by the standards given in chapter 5.

Confronting: Summarize a person's issue, noting discrepancies in her or his story. Decide which discrepancy needs to be challenged and why. Write both a mild and a direct confrontation statement. Evaluate your statements by the standards given in chapter 5.

Contending: Summarize a person's problem, noting the irrational belief that is part of the problem. Decide on the reasons and religious resources that you would use to dispute this belief and why you would use these. Formulate a statement or dialogue using these reasons and religious resources. Evaluate this contention using the standards in chapter 5.

2. Practicing Proclamation Skills in a Group

The pastor chooses a parishioner whom he or she is prepared to challenge. If the parishioner agrees to be challenged, the pastor offers a summary of what the pastor has seen the parishioner do and heard the parishioner say in relationship to the specific issue the pastor has chosen. This exercise can be done with either real life problems that have been shared in the group or role plays that have been done in the group.

For an example of this exercise, consider a pastor and parishioner who are seminary students taking a course –in pastoral care. The parishioner is a former college professor who has left her work to study for ordination.

The pastor says, "I have heard you talk about your grief about losing your status as an adult by becoming a student again. You have said that being reduced to this status has made you very angry. You tied this anger in with several issues—your difficulty in worship, the lateness of your papers, and the difficulty you have with the way this course is taught. Is that the way you remember it?"

In the exercise, after the pastor and parishioner negotiate a summary of the issue, the pastor uses one of the proclamation skills. Then the pastor helps the parishioner explore the challenge. When about five minutes have passed the pastor invites the parishioner to review his or her understanding.

The observer helps the parishioner first and then the pastor debrief. All three parties should discuss their reactions to the challenge. Especially important are feeling reactions to the proclamation and analyses of the strengths and weaknesses of its presentation. The observer should take care to help pastor and parishioner focus on the skill, and not continue discussing the parishioner's issue.

3. Practicing Proclamation Skills on Yourself

Begin by choosing an issue to dialogue with yourself about. After you have explored the issue with yourself in a written dialogue (you may use exercise 4A in chapter 3), challenge yourself using the proclamation skills. Finish with a review.

When you have finished writing your dialogue, reflect on it by answering these questions in writing: How do I feel about the problem or joy after doing this exercise? What insights have I gained or deepened by doing this?

Conclude by checking your "pastor" responses against the standards for each skill in chapter 5 and the descriptions of proclamation, condemnation, and abdication. Write down the insights you gained about your use of the proclamation skills.

6

Resources for Change

SEVEN RELIGIOUS RESOURCES are the skilled pastor's primary resources for change. The pastoral person, Scripture, tradition, theology and ethics, covenant communities, prayer and the arts, and rites are the distinctive means that pastors use to help parishioners change their distressing feelings and behaviors through changing their unhelpful beliefs.

Though the resources are presented more fully in this chapter, it is not alone in emphasizing their use. Scripture and theology were employed to fashion arguments for disputing unhelpful beliefs in chapters 4 and 5. Likewise, chapter 7 presents strategies for guiding parishioners in designing action plans that include these resources. This chapter begins with a pastoral theology of change, then discusses the religious resources, and concludes with an exploration of the pastoral use of the resources.

A PASTORAL THEOLOGY OF CHANGE

The power to change our understandings is a gift of the Holy Spirit that we are called to cooperate with and appropriate. For example, the Johannine Jesus emphasizes the gift aspect by telling the disciples that the Spirit "will teach you everything" and "guide you into all the truth" (John 14:25; 16:13). On the other hand the Pauline epistles exhort Christians to cooperate and appropriate: "Be transformed by the renewing of your minds" (Rom. 12:2) and "Be renewed in the spirit of your minds" (Eph. 4:23). This tension between change as a gift and change as something we have to work at is illustrated by the Pentecost story in Acts 2.

Three Thousand Baptized

According to Luke these baptisms took place in Jerusalem on the day of Pentecost, a Jewish celebration about fifty days after the Passover. The city was crowded with pilgrims who had come to observe the holy day. The disciples had been together praying for many days. On Pentecost the disciples were filled with the Holy Spirit and began to speak in tongues, which allowed them to be understood by the pilgrims each in her or his own language. This amazed the crowd and caused the people to wonder. Peter took this occasion to dispute their unhelpful beliefs about Jesus and to proclaim the gospel. Many of the listeners were "cut to the heart" and they asked, "What should we do?" "Peter said to them, 'Repent [*metanoia*] and be baptized . . . in the name of Jesus Christ so that your sins will be forgiven; and you will receive the gift of the Holy Spirit.' " Three thousand accepted the message and were baptized. These then "devoted themselves to the apostles' teaching and fellowship, to the breaking of bread and the prayers" (Acts 2:37, 38, 42).

In this story from Acts 2, change is both a gift of the Spirit and something people work at. The hearers are convinced of the truth of Peter's message by the Spirit, which "cuts them to the heart" and inspires them to ask, "What shall we do?" Yet they have to act to fully receive the gifts; Peter informs them that they must be baptized so that their sins will be forgiven and that they may receive the Holy Spirit. After baptism they continue to be engaged in activities that solidify their change: listening to the apostles' teaching, participating in the fellowship, celebrating the Lord's Supper, and attending the daily prayers at the temple.

The story of the baptism of the three thousand also contains the antecedents of the religious resources. The Scripture can be understood as the apostles' teaching. Tradition and contemporary theology and ethics that expound Scripture are extensions of that teaching. The apostles' fellowship is carried on by the pastoral person and the covenant community. Prayer is a continuation of their daily prayers in the temple. The rites find their source in Baptism and the breaking of bread.

Thus, the story of the baptism of the three thousand illustrates both the roles of inspiration and effort in changing perceptions and the importance of the religious resources in initiating and sustaining new understandings.

The Difficulty of Change

It is very difficult to change one's behavior; it makes no difference whether the behavior is covert (thoughts) or overt (actions). Therefore, people try to avoid changing their behavior. Cavanagh (1982, 240–50) lists four major reasons why people who seek help resist change. First, seeking help is anxiety-producing and painful. Second, it is complex. Third, the old behavior performed important functions for the one seeking help. Fourth, some of the reasons that caused a person to seek help are not supportive of change.

Seeking help causes anxiety and pain. Change is anxiety-producing and painful because parishioners must engage in two frightening activities: letting go of the old ways of dealing with their anxieties and facing their fears as they develop new ways. Both of these activities are uncomfortable. For example, Father Shaun Casey has always felt uncomfortable as an administrator because he believes that he must make everybody like him, and administrators have to make decisions that upset people. He feels his stomach tighten and sees all kinds of frightening images flash through his mind as he talks to his counselor about the possibility of facing people who are angry at his decisions.

Change is complex. Change is complex because parishioners have to both stop old behaviors (covert and overt) and start new ones. Letting go of the old and starting the new are complicated procedures, and combining them multiplies the complexity. Nancy Fratello wanted to spend more time praying, but as she searched for time she realized that she was overcommitted because she kept saying yes to people so that they would like her. In order to get that time she would have to wrestle with the irrational belief that everybody must like her, accept God's acceptance as enough, develop priorities so that she would know which people to say no to, develop ways to say no to people, change her schedule, develop ways to sustain herself through the discomfort of change, practice the new schedule, and get used to the longer prayer times.

Old behaviors are important. The behaviors that parishioners have to give up are important to their personal dynamics. They fulfill psychological needs, provide distraction, vent anger, and atone for guilt. Both Shaun and Nancy developed their belief that they must make everyone like them as small children who coped by appeasing dysfunctional parents. They have used this method of relating ever since and it has been successful in making them well liked and in providing distraction from their anxieties.

Poor motives for change inhibit change. Parishioners often enter the process with poor motives such as to get permission not to change, to validate a previously made decision, to prove someone else is to blame, to vent hostility on another, to manipulate others, to prove they are beyond help, to defeat the pastor, or to satisfy others. Not one of these motives supports positive change. Demetrius Papadopolous brought his wife, Alexandra, to see the pastor so that they could get their marriage turned around. Father Petros soon concluded that Demetrius had come to find an ally to support his point of view and that Alexandra was just going through the motions because she felt that the marriage was beyond help.

In sum, metanoia is hard even when we want it because there is always a part of us that does not want to be altered. This ambivalence is the major impediment to parishioners' accepting the gospel in stage 2 and carrying out their plans in stage 3. The difficulty of change and the universality of ambivalence are two the reasons that the accounts in Acts 2 of the baptism of the three thousand and their subsequent activities are so amazing.

Irrational Beliefs

Because of the many reasons that change is difficult, people often believe it is impossible. Thus, they do not work on the beliefs behind their distressing feelings and behaviors. One or both of the following irrational ideas are often behind this type of hopelessness: emotional irresponsibility and historical determinism.

Emotional irresponsibility.   That emotional misery comes from external pressures and that one has little ability to control or change one's feelings is *emotional irresponsibility.* This belief takes the truth that we usually respond with certain emotions to particular external situations and draws the false conclusion that the external situation causes the misery. Rather, our beliefs about the situation, such as: I can't stand it, It's absolutely awful and shouldn't happen, and It will be a catastrophe if it happens, upset us. The proof of this assertion is shown when we successfully dispute these ideas and our feelings do change. Though feelings are difficult to change, they can be transformed eventually.

According to Mark, Jesus' central message was the call to repentance (Mark 1:14-15). This call illustrates Jesus' belief that we can change our behaviors and are not simply slaves to outside pressures.

Historical determinism.   This is the idea that your past remains all-important and that because something once strongly influenced your life, it has to keep determining your feelings and behavior today.

The past, especially our time as a child in a family, has a strong influence on us. This influence is hard to break because we continue to practice in the present the behaviors and thoughts we learned in the past (for example, Father Shaun Casey and Nancy Fratello in the examples above). It is the present rehearsal, however, that continues the past's power. We can weaken old patterns by practicing new ones.

We see an example of this struggle in John 5. Jesus asked the man who had lain by the pool for thirty-eight years if he wished to be healed. The man responded by telling him about past failures. Jesus answered by inviting and empowering him to stand up in the present.

In sum, emotional irresponsibility and historical determinism are examples of the erroneous belief that humans are not free; they maintain that we are determined by outside pressures or historical precedents or both. In contrast, Christian theology reminds us that we are, in a limited way, free. That is, we are free to respond in various ways to these pressures and precedents, yet we are limited because these histories, habitual reactions, and our physical makeup do influence us. Therefore, any attempt to act differently must take these influences in account. However, the more that we practice acting against these influences, the better we get at exercising our freedom.

Resistance, Creaturehood, and Sin

The psychological disciplines call our opposition to change *resistance*. Indicators of this resistance are the various methods and tactics that we use to avoid change. Theologians describe both the deep-seated fear of change and the binding power of habit—two aspects of our opposition—as part of being a creature. They call another aspect of the opposition—dealing with our feelings idolatrously by seeking easy relief instead of growthful resolution—sin. For us creatures and sinners, fear of new behaviors, holding onto old inappropriate behaviors, and harboring poor motives are what we bring to every situation, even when we try not to. Whether we call this opposition to change resistance, creatureliness, sin, or some combination of the three, it is a frustrating phenomenon for both pastors and parishioners. In sum, creaturehood and sinfulness make behavioral change difficult.

Support for Change

The metanoia model emphasizes three supports for change: social influence, problem-solving methods, and religious resources.

Social influence. Social influence is the power we give others to affect our feelings, thoughts, and behaviors. Jerome Frank (1974) observes that the more influence persons give healers, the more likely that they will be helped by the healers' ministrations. Many of the factors that increase influence, like physical attractiveness, respect for the helper's profession, common background or experiences with a parishioner, are givens that pastors either have or do not have. Other factors such as reputation for effectiveness and the ability to keep confidences are more under pastors' control but are not basic skills of the type treated in this book.

Two important means for developing pastors' social influence are discussed in this book—helping skills and religious resources. The correct use of helping skills, particularly attending and responding, communicates pastors' care and competence and thus builds influence with parishioners. One of the main reasons that the presence skills are so important is that they enhance the pastoral relationship and thus make the subsequent proclamation and guidance more effective. Likewise, skill at utilizing the religious resources shows pastors' trustworthiness and competence. Parishioners often come to pastors specifically to have their issues considered from a religious perspective; they understand pastors' ability to meet this expectation as an indication of their competence. Because change is so difficult it is crucial that pastors use appropriate methods to develop enough social influence to be helpful.

For example, Father Petros worked hard to suppress his initial judgments and concentrate on first listening to Demetrius and Alexandra and then helping them listen to each other during the first hour of their meeting. After this, they were ready to deal with Petros's challenges and guidance during the final half hour.

Problem-solving methods.   Strategies for managing our concerns are problem-solving methods. The strategy presented in chapter 7, "Guidance Skills," includes: setting concrete goals, developing a program to reach these goals, and planning implementation of the program. This method helps parishioners deal with the difficulties of change by creating an action plan that breaks down the complex process of change into simple steps they are rewarded for taking. Father Shaun had thought that it would be impossible for him to change his habit of always trying to please everyone. He was surprised to see how much freer he felt after completing several simple steps of an action plan that he and his counselor had worked out.

Religious resources.   Religious resources speak to our difficulty with change in three important ways. First, they minister the presence of Christ to our deep-seated anxiety. They help us cope with dread by either relieving it or giving meaning to it or both, thus enabling us to endure the emotional cost of change. Second, these resources teach us the gospel beliefs that liberate us to trust God and see possibility in change. Third, such resources as the pastoral person, the covenant community, and the rites offer social support for change. For example, Nancy Fratello struggled with her program to have more prayer time until she finally worked a weekend prayer retreat into her schedule. There amidst the beauty of the woods, with much time and silence to pray through the Scripture readings assigned by the retreat director, and inspired by the powerful worship, she found the strength to combat her irrational belief by making some tough choices and detailed plans.

SEVEN RELIGIOUS RESOURCES

The seven religious resources are pastors' primary tools for helping parishioners change. The pastoral person, Scripture, tradition, contemporary theology and ethics, prayer and the arts, covenant communities, and the rites are well-attested opportunities for experiencing the transforming love, power, and wisdom of God. As illustrated by the discussion of the baptism of the three thousand, they were used to engender and sustain change from the beginning of the church. Though their use has been introduced throughout this book, this is the section in which they are discussed most fully.

Pastoral Persons

Pastoral persons represent God and the church and are responsible for communicating the good news by word and deed. Pastors are the key resource because they provide the context for the others. As stated earlier, the fundamental contribution pastors make is the quality of the relationship. This is a major factor in parishioners' acceptance of pastors' proclamation and guidance. The unique role of pastors is theological assessment, which gives direction to the use of the other religious resources. Pastors have the responsibility of tailoring the gospel to parishioners' particular issues, beliefs, and ways of hearing.

Scripture, Tradition, and
Theology and Ethics

Scripture, tradition, and contemporary *theology and ethics* are three resources that can be grouped together because all three are written proclamations of the good news. The Scripture contains the basic statements and stories of the good news by which all others are measured. Christian tradition provides instructive examples of persons and groups whose lives and teachings illustrate the gospel in various ages, cultures, and situations. Contemporary theology and ethics proclaim the good news in the language of our time and culture. The basic technique for the personal use of these three resources is meditation.

Since the term *meditation* is used differently in Christian tradition than in modern secular (and some modern religious) writing, I will use the following definition (J. Neville Ward 1983, 85): "In Meditation the mind reflects on some Christian truth or passage of scripture or personal experience using words or ideas in more or less logical progression, with the aim of reaching fuller understanding and personal appropriation of the truth considered, or working through some experience in the life of Christian faith in order to come to some decision, awareness of God's will or reaffirmation of faith."

Meditation on Scripture, tradition, and contemporary theology and ethics is a way of allowing the Good News to sink deeply into our souls, digging up our irrational beliefs and planting images of God's extravagant love, liberating power, and invigorating invitation to imitate that love in relating to others.

All of Scripture can be used for meditation. Parts of tradition often used for meditation are: stories of great Christian lives, teachings of the important theologians, sayings of the spiritual masters, and hymns, poems, prayers, and rites. Contemporary writing on theology and ethics can be read meditatively, also, to help understand the Christian story from an up-to-date viewpoint. Popular religious books and devotional manuals are included in this category, along with more academic works.

Prayer

This category of *prayer* includes various types of prayer, spiritual disciplines, techniques, devotional materials, and arts (poetry, music, drama, visual arts, etc.) that support individual and corporate awareness of God's presence, love, and call. This discussion, however, is limited to six types of prayer.

The personal prayer of parishioners is a vital resource. Prayer relates them to God at the level that deals directly with the intense anxiety that sustains ambivalence. Prayer is the proper context for dealing with opposition to change because it puts God in the center of the whole process. The side effects of putting God in the center often include (1) making parishioners more receptive to the action of God's transforming love and power; and (2) reducing anxiety about change by moving the locus of trust from parishioners' wills and capabilities to God's faithfulness.

Each type of prayer contributes a unique kind of support to the change process. Adoration and praise sustain and deepen parishioners' personal relationships with God, which in turn sustains them through the desert of anxiety. Petition for strength to do the required step and intercession for those who will be helped by their actions set a context for implementation of the action plan. Prayers of thanksgiving when a step is made, and confession when one is missed, set the context for evaluation of progress in moving toward the goals.

In addition to the five types of prayer discussed above there is another that is very important in supporting behavioral change—contemplation. According to Ward (1983, 85), "Contemplation, in its Christian uses . . . denotes the kind of prayer in which the mind does not function discursively but is arrested in a simple attention and one-pointedness."

Various forms of breath prayer, centering prayer, and the Jesus Prayer, as well as nondiscursive attentiveness to works of Christian art are acts of contemplation. These contemplative practices deepen our relationship to God and have the side benefits of reducing anxiety, developing our ability to tolerate distressing feelings, and opening our awareness to new possibilities.

Covenant Communities

Covenant communities are groups of two or more Christians who provide support for living according to the gospel. Its members are bound together to support the decision to change, to give clear feedback, and to model the new life. For example, pastor and parishioner form a small covenant community. The importance of covenant communities comes from the power of social influence in affecting behavior. The people to whom we relate vulnerably—spouse, family, friends, support group, prayer group, counselors—affect the way we see the world, what we value, and how we act on these beliefs. Therefore it is important to build a covenant community into any plan for change.

At times the social support of non-Christians can be helpful in supporting change because of their expertise or the compatibility of their understandings. The twelve-step programs (Alcoholics Anonymous, Alanon, Narcotics Anonymous, etc.) providing intensive social support for a change of behavior and thought based on spiritual principles are an example of a helpful group that is not specifically Christian.

Rites

Rites are rituals (e.g., Baptism, Eucharist, marriage, and burial) that combine the other resources into one multilayered statement of the gospel.

Participation in them provides a combination of many of the benefits of the other resources. For example, the worshiper at Eucharist (Holy Communion, Lord's Supper, or Mass) usually receives pastoral persons' insights in a homily or sermon; the support of the covenant community; a chance to meditate on Scripture, tradition, and contemporary theology and ethics as they are presented in readings and ritual prayers; an invitation to adore and praise, intercede, petition, confess, and give thanks; and an opportunity to contemplate.

The rite's interplay of words, actions, symbols, and pastoral presence communicates the good news powerfully, often working where single resources do not. An example of this is reconciliation (penance, private confession, confessional conversation) in which a person confesses to God in the presence of a pastor. It has been my experience, and the experience of many others, that this combination of pastoral person, Scripture, tradition, and prayer communicates God's forgiveness when both private and public prayer have been ineffective. Another example is the healing rites (unction, ministry to the sick, healing service, etc.), which often include Scripture reading, prayers for healing, laying on of hands, and anointing with oil. These rites are often experienced as more effective in healing than simple prayer, receiving communion, reading Scripture, or discussing a problem in depth.

The rites incorporate all of the other resources and present them with power. They empower the pastoral person; they communicate Scripture, tradition, and theology; they nourish and instruct personal prayer, and they call together and build up community. Some of the rites, such as personal devotions (private prayer, psalms, and Scripture reading), are to be used daily as a means of nourishing private prayer by relating it to the Scripture, tradition, and theology. Personal devotions join one to all Christians who are praying around the world. Such rites are resources to be used as a regular part of an action plan.

Some rites are celebrated less frequently, and are, therefore, used as the centerpiece for an action plan—something one prepares for, celebrates, and reflects upon. The marriage rite is an example of a centerpiece rite. The process of preparing for, celebrating, and reflecting upon this rite is intended to support the couple in adopting the new behavior that marriage requires. The celebration of the rite is intended to involve them in a covenant community and nourish their private prayer. The elements of tradition, Scripture, and theology in the rite provide material for meditation during the preparation for and the reflection upon the ceremony. The whole process relates the couple to one or more pastoral persons. Thus, this centerpiece rite can bring all of the religious resources into play.

These seven resources are powerful means for sustaining parishioners in their programs. Nevertheless, pastors should not force them on parishioners. The decision about which religious resources are to be used, if any, is dependent on parishioners' desires to use them.

Applying the Resources

Particular religious resources are especially suited to disputing the irrational beliefs related to despair, dread, or alienation. This section gives direction in relating resources to one of these assessment categories. The listing below should be read, however, with the understanding that both human souls and God's grace are wonderful and mysterious. Thus, neither can be captured completely by the logic and research that created this list. Further, the information below is meant to be suggestive, not exhaustive.

Despair. Despair is the low self-esteem, shame, self- and other blame that comes from not accepting God's mercy. The resources and practices that address it are those that help parishioners experience their acceptance. These include

- rite of confession (penance, reconciliation)
- confessional conversation with a pastoral person
- participating in a covenant community in which sharing of struggles is encouraged and an atmosphere of acceptance is maintained
- study and meditation on the good news of God's mercy in Scripture, tradition, contemporary theology and ethics
- focusing on experiences of acceptance and affirmation during prayer (thanksgiving) or writing in a journal
- prayers of confession
- forgiving others as a spiritual discipline
- acts of restitution
- prayers for inner healing or the healing of memories.

Dread. Dread is terror in the face of powerlessness and death. Dread comes from trusting in things that pass away. It is disputed by resources and practices that shift the focus from the fearful possibilities to trust in and enjoyment of God's presence, creation, and power:

- corporate worship
- contemplation

- prayers of praise and adoration
- recreation, play, leisure, and exercise (practical ways of taking delight in God's creation)
- study and meditation on the power of God as expressed in creation, the deliverance of Israel, Jesus' resurrection, the lives of the saints in Scripture and tradition, the second coming.

Alienation.   Alienation is care deformed into self-protection by fear of the future, guilt about the past, and frustration in the present. Resources and practices that focus on self-giving or counteract frustration dispute alienation. Some of these are

- commissioning rites: baptism and the rites that apply the baptismal ministry to particular circumstances (i.e., confirmation, marriage, ordination, and various lay ministries)
- involvement in the covenant community's mission
- prayers of intercession and petition
- prayers of thanksgiving (the antidote to frustration)
- resources that deal with underlying despair or dread (see above)
- study and meditation on Jesus as model, the call to discipleship and ministry, forgiveness and reconciliation in Scripture, tradition, and theology and ethics.

The items in these lists are broad categories. It is the job of the parishioner and pastor to work out particular practices that fit these general outlines. For instance, a despairing person may decide to meditate on Rom. 5:8 ("But God proves his love for us in that while we still were sinners Christ died for us"). The form of the meditation would have to be determined by the parishioner's experience and needs. When resources are adapted to the parishioners' issues and experience they are powerful ways of disputing irrational beliefs.

PREPARING FOR PASTORAL USE

By pastoral use I mean utilizing the religious resources to help another. In addition to practice in pastoral use, there are two ways to develop abilities to use these resources pastorally: academic study and personal practice. Academic study of the resources is researching their meaning and deployment. Personal use, by contrast, consists of employing them as "means of grace," tools God uses to transform us into more loving persons. Putting the resources to use for personal change distinguishes personal practice from pastoral use or academic study. Both academic study and personal practice are discussed in this section.

Academic Study

Academic study of the religious resources is important because their meaning, and therefore application, is not always obvious. Because pastors use the resources in informing and contending they need to know how various resources communicate the gospel. For example, Mary Peterson and John King met with Peter Johnson, the pastor of a church near their campus, to prepare for their wedding. Mary and John are serious Christians who have been part of a Bible fellowship while in college. They told the pastor that they want to have a Christian marriage. They had been reading Ephesians 5 as preparation and had an argument about the meaning of verse 22, "Wives, be subject to your husbands as you are to the Lord." Peter Johnson's response to them depends on his understanding of two questions: What does the verse mean? How are we to respond to it today?

What does the verse mean? For a long time the commentators seemed to agree that it meant that wives were to submit themselves to husbands in a way that was very different from the way that husbands were to relate to them. Now there are responsible commentators who read this verse differently. Utilizing modern research into New Testament Greek grammar, word usage, forms, and historical context, they understand verse 22 to be one illustration of verse 21, "Be subject to one another out of reverence for Christ." According to this point of view, verse 25, "Husbands, love your wives, just as Christ loved the church and give himself up for her" is the parallel illustration of submission (Garland and Garland, 1986, chap. 2). Thus, a very simple, clear statement may not be simple or clear at all. Pastor Johnson had to decide through study what the verse meant.

He had to come up with a response, also, to the second and more difficult question: How are we to respond to it today? Various answers to these questions are related to the answer to a methodological question, What is the relative importance of tradition, contemporary reason, and contemporary experience in interpreting Scripture for our times?

Academic study is important because, as we have seen in our example, there are various answers to these questions depending on the approach pastors take. Pastors need to study and develop carefully the approach for both counseling others and their personal use. Such research should include investigation into their own approach as well as those of others in order to be equipped to respond to various pastoral situations.

Personal Practice

As stated above, personal practice consists of employing religious resources as means of grace, tools God uses to transform us into more loving persons. They support this change in at least three ways: (1) they minister the presence of Christ to sustain us through the anxiety of growth; (2) they dispute our irrational ideas and teach us gospel beliefs; and (3) some of them (pastoral persons, covenant community, rites) offer social support. In their personal practice, pastors use the means of grace differently from the way parishioners do.

One factor that often affects personal practice is involvement in academic study. The purpose of study is to provide information for practice. The logic is, the better we understand what the resources mean the more we will be able to apply them to our lives. Thus, continuing the example above, the more Peter understood about Ephesians 5, the marriage text of the Book of Common Prayer, and contemporary understandings of marriage, the better able he would be to integrate them into his own prayer and marriage.

Further, personal practice adds the knowledge and authority that comes from experience to academic study. Our ability confidently to recommend religious resources and correctly to prescribe their use is largely dependent on our personal practice. Extending the example cited above, Peter Johnson's experience of trying to live in a relationship based on the Ephesians passage, the Book of Common Prayer marriage service, the canons, and contemporary insights about marriage adds a dimension to his understanding of these sources.

Pastors' use of Scripture, tradition, theology, and ethics is often affected by academic study, because the critical approach interferes with meditation—at first. This phenomenon is analogous to that of the process of learning the helping skills (described in chap. 2 above), in which the move from being unconscious of limited competence to being conscious of limited competence is disconcerting. Similarly, students are disoriented by moving from a rudimentary knowledge of the Bible in English to a critical knowledge of the historical context, sources, differences between the original and translations, and contrasting perspectives between the books of the Bible. However, just as the route to increased comfort in using the skills is through intense practice, so also the path to better meditation is more practice in study and prayer. One reward for this effort is that the greater our knowledge of Scripture or tradition or contemporary theology and ethics, the more likely our applications of that resource will be apt, and, conversely, the less likely they will be mistaken and simplistic.

Pastors who study the rites and their performance often experience difficulties similar to those that arise from the study of Scripture, tradition, and theology and ethics. The remedy is similar, also—increased participation in the rites until the critical perspective supports worship rather than detracts from it. For many, participation as a leader of the rites poses an additional distraction because so much is required. Detailed prior planning of the service, rehearsals, and prayerful preparation of the leaders are three strategies to enable worship by those who preside.

Many pastors like to help others but do not allow themselves to be taken care of. Thus, pastors avoid utilizing pastoral persons. It is important to use this resource because the helpfulness of pastoring is related to pastors' experiences of being helped. Pastoral persons help each other in several ways. First, being pastored teaches pastors how it feels to be a parishioner—thus developing empathy. Second, the other pastor's feedback helps pastors to become more aware of that part of themselves that is more visible to others than to ourselves. Third, pastors help each other experience God's acceptance by their acceptance of each other. They offer aid in a fourth way by assisting each other to face those issues that are difficult to face. Experience in working with these issues contributes greatly to the wisdom and authority pastors bring to assisting others. Three areas in which pastors can use pastoral persons to improve pastoral skills are supervision of pastoral work, guidance in prayer and vocation, and reflection on personal crises.

Covenant communities. Covenant communities help in many of the ways that pastoral persons do; and many pastors have similar difficulties with using them. Communities of three or more, however, have several advantages over the two-person pastor-parishioner group. One is that they provide more opportunities for feedback. A second and related advantage is that they provide more people on which to project (to ascribe to another person feelings and thoughts that are resident but unacknowledged in oneself). That is, in a group there are often persons whom we like or dislike intensely because we project on them feelings, thoughts, and attitudes that we need to work on. When the group feedback helps us to see that the issue is ours and not the other person's, we become much more aware of these qualities in ourselves, thus growing in self-awareness and self-acceptance. In addition, the process of learning to cooperate with a group of people is practice in empathy and respect—a third benefit of the covenant community. The practice group is the basic covenant community that helps pastors develop their skills. Supervisory groups and colleague support groups are other important covenant communities for pastors.

Prayer.   Prayer is a powerful resource for opening pastors up to God's transforming love and power. Though each category of prayer makes a contribution to the relationship with God, which is the foundation of pastors' self-awareness and self-acceptance, I limit my discussion to two that I have found to have peculiar relevance in the development of skilled pastors—contemplation and intercession.

Contemplation.   There is considerable psychological research on the effects of nonreligious forms of contemplation on counselors. (Note: Much nonreligious writing calls the practice of nondiscursive attentiveness meditation.) Carrington (1982) summarizes this research by noting that contemplation significantly increases the empathic ability of counselors in terms of sensitivity to nonverbals, ability to be attentive for long hours, tolerance of patient's negative reactions, and awareness of patient's issues.

The practice of Christian forms of contemplation seems to have similar benefits for those who practice it on a regular basis. We have found that a daily practice of contemplative prayer improves pastors' ability to be empathetic. The benefits of this practice can be brought into a particular conversation by taking time for a minute or so of contemplative prayer immediately before a pastoral conversation. In sum, contemplation is practicing being present to God and it prepares pastors to be present to others.

Intercession.   Intercession is important for pastors for several reasons. First, it transforms vision; through intercession pastors begin to see parishioners in God's light, rather than in the dark shadows of human valuation. Second, intercession bonds pastors to parishioners because praying for people deepens their care for them. The power of prayer to help others is the third reason for this practice. Whereas these first two reasons show that intercession liberates pastors' caring, the third points to its help to parishioners. All together indicate that intercession is a powerful means of exercising care. Students have found this to be true by praying daily for the other members of their practice groups.

In sum, personal practice of the religious resources should be a part of the training and regular discipline of pastors because it is a means of experiencing the good news that changes us into more effective pastors.

LEARNING THE SKILLS

This chapter has discussed the seven religious resources as tools for helping parishioners change the understandings that result in distressing feelings and behaviors. It has done this by putting forth a pastoral theology of change, describing the resources and their application, and explaining the ways to prepare for their use.

The basic thesis of the pastoral theology of change is that the power to change is a gift of the spirit that pastors and parishioners must work to accept. Attempts to appropriate this gift are frustrated by creaturehood and sinfulness. Thus the metanoia model uses social influence, problem-solving methods, and religious resources to support those efforts.

Social influence and problem-solving methods are used by a variety of helpers but Scripture, tradition, contemporary theology and ethics, covenant communities, prayer, and rites are the unique tools of pastoral persons. Therefore pastors need to engage in academic study and personal practice to prepare themselves to use these unique tools.

Exercise

Practicing the Personal Use of Religious Resources

Choose one of your issues that has been worked through stage 2 (for instance, the issue you used for exercise 3 in chap. 5). Pick a written prayer or a passage of Scripture that expresses the gospel belief that you need to rehearse. Read the prayer or Scripture meditatively for several minutes each day for two weeks. At the end of two weeks record the effects this practice has had on both your perspective and the issue.

7

Guidance

PARISHIONERS' STAGE 3 TASK is developing and implementing a plan to change their thoughts (covert behavior) and actions (overt behavior) so that they can better manage their problems and celebrate their joys. Because constructing and carrying out action plans is difficult, pastors use *guidance* skills to support parishioners in their efforts.

The three guidance skills are: setting goals, developing programs, and planning implementation. ①*Setting goals* is choosing a specific objective and stating it in terms that are measurable, manageable, and meaningful. ②*Developing programs* is making a plan to accomplish the goal and involves: choosing steps, scheduling them, and creating reinforcements. ③*Planning implementation* is preparing to carry out the program, which includes reviewing the program, and, if necessary, rehearsing and revising it.

The guidance skills build on the presence and proclamation skills. The work pastors do in stage 3 is based on the relationship and information that result from using the presence skills in stage 1 and the new perspective that results from using the proclamation skills in stage 2. Further, presence and proclamation skills are used in carrying out the tasks of guidance. Pastors employ presence skills to explore the content and feelings of the statements that parishioners make while developing and implementing an amendment plan. Likewise, pastors utilize proclamation skills to challenge any perspectives that interfere with the tasks of setting goals, developing programs, and planning implementation.

The following continuation of the supervisory conversation begun in chapter 5 between Doris Thomas, who supervises the lay visitors program, and Sam Peters, a lay visitor, illustrates the use of the guidance skills and the use of presence and proclamation skills in stage 3.

THE VOICE OF PAIN

In the earlier part of this conversation Sam complained that he was having trouble visiting James, a dying parishioner. As Doris and Sam discussed the problem it became clear to Doris that the real problem was Sam's idolatrous belief that feeling pain while ministering was an indication that he was not a good visitor. Doris reminded Sam that Jesus had experienced pain while ministering and that she and a lot of ministers have that same experience. This part of the verbatim begins by repeating Sam's last statement from the previous verbatim.

Conversation

SAM: Well . . . I feel better about myself because I'm not the only one that experiences pain when I try to minister . . . and . . . the thing about my ideas making the problem worse . . . both were helpful. What I want to know now is how do I deal with this voice I keep hearing?

DORIS: What comes to your mind?

SAM: Not much.

DORIS: How have you dealt with such voices in the past?

SAM: I don't know . . . I guess, let me see . . . I used to have those voices whenever I flew. At first, I was real nervous when I got into an airplane. But I kept on flying—I had to because my job required that I do some long-distance travel—and after a while, it stopped bothering me so much. I guess I just kept going in spite of the voices and gradually they pretty much went away.

DORIS: So one of the ways you have dealt with such voices is by continuing to act in spite of them.

SAM: Yeah.

DORIS: Did you ever talk to yourself as a way of dealing with the voices?

SAM: Come to think of it, I used to keep telling myself all that stuff about how much safer flying was than driving. And I would look around at all the other people on the plane and say to myself, They're dealing with it, you can too.

DORIS: So in addition to going ahead and flying despite the voices, you also disputed the voices by repeating opposing ideas.

SAM: Yeah. And it worked, too. [*Said with energy*] Now, I hardly worry about it at all. [Doris says, "Huh."] [*Pause*] I would like visiting James to be like that.

DORIS: Your goal is to have your concern about the voice that says you shouldn't have pain when visiting James diminish like the voices that used to bother you while flying.

SAM: Uh-huh, that's exactly it. I would like to know that I was conquering this the way I conquered that.

DORIS: How would you measure that? What would you like to have happen by when so you can tell how you are doing?

SAM: That's a tough one. How do you measure the voices and how do you set a goal date?

DORIS: Yes, it is tough, but it's important that you choose a target date and a measurement so you can tell if you are making progress.

SAM: OK. How about this—by a month from now I want to be less bothered by the voice. Is that a good enough target date and measurement? I can't think of a more precise one.

DORIS: By a month from now, you want to feel less bothered by the voice. That sounds specific enough. Does it feel right to you?

SAM: Yeah. It feels all right.

DORIS: How would you go about reducing the voice?

SAM: Well, I guess I would do the same thing as I did about flying. I would visit James twice as much [weekly instead of every two weeks] and I would keep telling myself what you said about pain that I am experiencing—it does not prove that I am a bad visitor. I would just try to remember that Jesus was pained in the garden, but he accepted it. And that other pastors feel the same way.

DORIS: How do you plan to remind yourself of that?

SAM: I don't know, I hadn't thought about that.

DORIS: What would be a good way of reminding yourself of that?

SAM: Well, I could do what I did about flying. Whenever the thought comes up—I would just remind myself about Jesus and other pastors.

DORIS: Does that seem workable to you?

SAM: Yep.

DORIS: When will you evaluate how things are working? You know, what parts of the plan are working, what parts are not?

SAM: I was thinking about doing that at check-in time during our next three meetings. [The supervisory meetings are held every two weeks.]

DORIS: Sounds good. Would you please review your plan for me?

SAM: My goal is to have my reaction to the voice diminish some by the end of a month. I will help this by doubling my visits to James in spite of the voice, and by reminding myself that Jesus' experience and other pastors' experiences dispute the voice. And that's about it. Oh, yeah. I will let you and everybody know how it's going during check-in time.

DORIS: That sounds like a workable plan. How does it feel to you?

SAM: It feels really good to have a way to get at this thing. I feel better already. It's something I really want to do.

DORIS: OK. I look forward to hearing from you next meeting.

Analysis

This is a verbatim of stage 3 in a conversation. In it Doris, the pastor, guides Sam, the parishioner, in the process of developing an action plan to change his thoughts (covert behavior) about the meaning of the pain he feels when visiting James, a dying parishioner.

This portion of the conversation begins with Sam's invitation to move to stage 3. Doris probes to discover Sam's plan but he is not conscious of one. Doris tries another probe to help Sam become conscious of what he knows about action plans. This time Sam remembers. Doris paraphrases Sam's responses to help him explore and become more conscious of what he knows. This strategy helps Sam to begin to set a goal.

Doris and Sam then work on setting goals. Doris begins by paraphrasing so that Sam can hear and explore the goal he states, that he would like his visits to James to be worry-free. After Sam confirms her paraphrase, Doris probes to get Sam to make his goal more specific. He resists specificity, so Doris empathizes and then explains the need for specificity. Sam responds by articulating a specific goal of being less bothered by visiting James in one month. Doris repeats this goal to help both of them explore it, then she affirms, and finally probes to discern his feeling about the goal. Sam concludes the goal setting by stating that he feels all right about the goal.

Once the goal has been identified, Doris and Sam turn to program development. Doris invites Sam to consider developing a program with a probe. He responds by choosing the steps of visiting James weekly and disputing the voice by repeating Doris's proclamation that Jesus also underwent pain. Doris then probes to see what reinforcements Sam intends to use. Sam responds that he thinks the informal style that he used before will be enough. Doris decides not to push this further. She then suggests another type of reinforcement—evaluation—which Sam was thinking about and accepts.

The final interchanges are concerned with planning implementation. Doris asks Sam to review his plan to help him see whether or not it is workable. Sam recounts the plan accurately and expresses his excitement about it. Doris ends the conversation by expressing her interest in the coming evaluation—a way of both approving the plan and emphasizing the importance of the next evaluation.

A THEOLOGY OF GUIDANCE

The metanoia model's theology of guidance can be summed up in one phrase—the Holy Spirit is the guide. It is the Spirit not the pastor who has both the responsibility and the capability of inspiring and directing change (cf. John 14:26; 16:12-13; Gal. 5:22-23). This Holy Spirit speaks directly to persons and is revealed in some of their feelings, experiences, actions, and thoughts.

Because the Holy Spirit speaks directly to parishioners, pastors use their knowledge of religious resources and action planning to draw out, support, and enhance parishioners' plans. Normally, pastors do not use their skills to make plans for parishioners. In the example of Doris and Sam, Doris used her knowledge to ask the kind of questions that help him develop an action plan. She asked, "How would you measure that? How would you go about reducing the voice? How do you plan to remind yourself of that?" She only made one recommendation: "It is important that you choose a target date and a measurement so that you can tell if you are making progress."

An important technique for helping parishioners identify what the Spirit is telling them is asking questions such as: What do you think God is calling you to do in this situation? What is one specific thing you could do to act on that call? How have you dealt with similar situations before? What do you think your goal should be? How do you think you might achieve that goal? What has come up in your prayers about this? After parishioners have developed a goal or a plan or a reinforcement, it is important to ask them how it feels and does it fit. These questions are asked in certain hope that the Holy Spirit will help the pastor and parishioner discern God's call.

Pastors and parishioners can listen to the Spirit in confidence, trusting that the Spirit's plan will be tailored to parishioners' experiences, personalities, abilities, and circumstances. One way to tell that action plans are inspired by the Holy Spirit is that they fit parishioners, freeing them to act out of their true selves. Conversely, plans that are built out of dread or despair or alienation will oppress parishioners by forcing them to act in ways that are not suitable. In unholy plans, parishioners create more problems for themselves by trying to justify themselves, not dealing with the real issues out of dread or alienation, or acting in ways that are otherwise contrary to the gospel.

Doris Thomas's conversation with Sam Peters at the beginning of this chapter provides a model of inductive guidance. Doris began by asking

Sam what plans came to his mind. When Sam said not much she did not jump in with a plan; rather she asked more questions to help draw him out. Each time he came up with part of a plan she would paraphrase it to allow him to explore it. She would also ask him directly how the plan felt or if it fit. All of these were strategies to help Sam get in touch with the guidance that the Holy Spirit was giving him.

FACILITATIVE CONDITIONS

In stage 3 the parishioners have the task of developing and implementing a plan to change their thoughts and actions. Pastors take on the job of helping parishioners deal with the difficulty of change. Because of this each particular facilitative condition is valued and expressed differently from stage 2.

Concreteness

Concreteness is the key facilitative condition for the guidance skills because specificity makes plans more effective. Vagueness in goals or programs or implementation strategies makes these tools too dull to cut through the difficulty of change. That is, when we do not have clear detailed plans to do something new, it is easier to lapse back to the old that we know how to do. Further, fuzziness is often a symptom of our ambivalence about change. For instance, refusal to set a definite time, place, or procedure to do a task is an indication of at least partial unwillingness to get the job done.

In the conversation between Doris and Sam, Doris pushes Sam to be specific about his goal, his program, and his implementation strategy by asking pointed questions. Because concreteness is the key facilitative condition, Doris uses probes frequently in this stage. In addition, the probes she uses are closed as a way of demanding specificity.

Empathy

Empathy, entering into parishioners' frames of reference, continues to be important in this stage, but its focus is narrowed to the parishioners' feelings, experiences, actions, and thoughts related to action planning. Thus, as noted above, Doris is directive in her use of paraphrases and probes. She is trying to find out what Sam knows about changing his beliefs and how he feels about the plans they are making. These presence skills help both Sam and Doris hear what the Spirit is saying through Sam's thoughts and reactions.

Concreteness and empathy are used in both the action-planning conversation(s) and any follow-up conversations that take place. Respect and genuineness have their place in those latter conversations that evaluate and discuss parishioners' implementation of their plans.

Respect

Respect is very different in this stage because the focus of regard is parishioners' decisions to change. Therefore pastors communicate conditional regard—positive approval for acting on their decisions to change, and the withdrawal of this positive reinforcement when parishioners do not act on their decisions. It is conditional because an "if-then" pattern is set up: if parishioners do the steps they have chosen, then there will be approval; and if they do not, then the approval will be withheld.

Genuineness

Pastors are most fully *genuine* in stage 3. Pastors are freer to share their reactions (including conditional regard and pastors' experiences with behavioral change) to parishioners' goals, programs, and plans because pastors are helping parishioners carry out *their* plans—not the pastor's plans. Thus pastors do not have to hold back to keep from imposing their wills on parishioners. In fact, parishioners often need the force of pastors' reactions to support them in their decisions against the internal and external forces that oppose change.

Keeping in mind these guidelines for using the guidance skills—the Holy Spirit is the guide, and concreteness is the key facilitative condition in stage 3—we are ready to discuss setting goals, developing programs, and planning implementation.

SETTING GOALS

Setting goals is choosing a specific objective and stating it in terms that are measurable, manageable, and meaningful. Egan (1982, 105) defines a goal as "what a client wants to do or accomplish in order to manage a problem situation or some part of it more effectively." Goals are the pivotal element in the pastoral conversation. All of the exploring and all of the understanding are preparation for goal setting; all of the programs and planning are for implementation of the goal once set.

Choose a Specific Objective

Choosing a specific objective is important because goals give direction to programs. Some people think first of vague intents or general goals that are too broad to provide focus. The statement, "I need to do something about my ministry skills" is an example of a vague intent. "I would like to improve in pastoral care" is an example of a general goal. The first step of goal setting is developing a specific goal such as: I intend to improve my responding skills. This level of specificity makes it clear exactly what the program should help the pastor in this example do about ministry skills or to improve pastoral care.

Make It Achievable

The second step is to state this specific objective in terms that are measurable, manageable, and meaningful. These characteristics give further direction to program development.

Goals are *measurable* if they have specific time frames and their projected results are verifiable. For instance, the statement "I intend to improve my responding skills" is not considered measurable because of its nonspecific time frame and nonspecific objectives for improvement. The statement "By the end of the semester, I will have doubled the number of times that I reflect feelings in pastoral conversations" has the necessary measurability. Measurable goals help program planning and reinforcement creating by providing a time frame for the program and a means of evaluation for reinforcement.

Goals are *manageable* if they are owned by parishioners, if parishioners have the resources to accomplish them, and if they are within parishioners' control. If a parishioner perceives the goal to be imposed, then it is not owned. Goals that are not owned are usually either abandoned or carried out at the expense of parishioners' integrity and creativity.

A goal is not considered manageable if it requires more time, treasure, talent, or training than a parishioner has or can be reasonably expected to obtain with the goal's time frame. For example, the goal of "doubling the times one reflects feeling in pastoral conversations" in one semester is manageable if one is in a setting in which there is supervision and opportunity for practice.

A goal that is not within a parishioner's control is not considered manageable. For instance, a goal to make someone else like you is not manageable because control belongs to another person, whereas a goal of developing one's responding skills is manageable. Learning to respond well, which is under one's control, however, is a good strategy for increasing the chances that another person may like you.

Goals are *meaningful* if their accomplishment would help parishioners manage problem situations more effectively and if they are in concert with parishioners' values. For example, Wally and Diane Johnson want to spend more time with each other. They find that the goal of getting up an hour earlier every day to have more time is not effective because they are so tired that they fall asleep an hour earlier at night, before they complete their evening child-care and household duties. A goal of giving their three children away would be an effective way to free more time with each other but it is absurdly against their values—they are deeply committed to raising their children.

Developing goals that are measurable, manageable, and meaningful is hard work; thus, pastors and parishioners must fight temptations to settle for vague intents rather than specific goals. Poorly developed goals are one major cause for the failure of programs to amend lives. Thus, responsible goal setting is worth the time and trouble it takes.

Finally, setting goals is an exercise in acceptance, hope, and love. It is a sign of contrition because sorrow that results in changed behavior signals acceptance of God's love. Setting goals is also a statement of hope because it witnesses to one's belief that change is possible. Behavior that needs change usually adversely affects one's ministry. Making a start toward changing that behavior is an act of love for the neighbor.

DEVELOPING PROGRAMS

Developing programs is making a plan to accomplish the goal. When the goal is specific, the program develops directly from it. The goal used in the previous sections: "By the end of the semester, I will have doubled the number of times that I reflect feelings in pastoral conversations" leads directly to a program. That goal provides a time frame (the end of the semester), a specific project (to learn to reflect feelings more), and criteria for evaluation (double the number of times)—three basic items for constructing a program.

There are three basic tasks in developing a program: choosing steps, scheduling steps, and creating reinforcements.

Choosing Steps

The basic units of programs are *steps*. Steps are separable tasks that lead to the accomplishment of the goal. These steps, like the goal, must be measurable, manageable, and meaningful. For instance, choosing steps, scheduling, and creating reinforcements are all steps toward developing programs. Counting the number of times one reflects feelings now, learning about reflecting feelings, practicing reflecting feelings, are all steps toward the goal of "doubl[ing] the number of times that I reflect feelings."

It is important to have small achievable steps so that parishioners can walk steadily toward the goal without having to take long dangerous leaps. Achieving a step strengthens hope by making the distance to the goal seem less formidable. Therefore complex steps (made up of several smaller tasks) should be broken down into substeps. As an example, the step of learning about reflecting feelings could be broken down into three substeps: learning to identify feelings, learning how to reflect, and learning when to reflect feelings.

Brainstorming is the process of thinking up steps. In brainstorming it is important to allow parishioners to toss out ideas without censure. The idea behind brainstorming is that the wildest idea may lead to a helpful one. For example, the idea of giving their three children away came to Wally in a brainstorm. This idea, absurd as it is, led to the helpful, workable idea of leaving the children in day-care an hour longer each day.

After the ideas are put forth it is time to *evaluate* them for measurability, manageability, and meaningfulness. This is the time that the appropriateness of the ideas is considered.

Scheduling

Scheduling is the process of sequencing steps and assigning times to start and finish them. Steps are usually sequenced by deciding which step must be done in order to do the other steps. In the example of doubling the times one reflects feelings, learning how to reflect feelings would come before practicing reflecting feelings.

Assigning start and finish times to the steps involves two estimations: how long a step takes and how much of the total program time it should take. If one decides to double the number of times one reflects feelings in pastoral conversation in one semester, then how long does it take to learn to identify feelings, how much of the semester should be devoted to this step, and how much time to the other steps? Assigning times makes it easier for parishioners and pastors to either see and celebrate the completion of a step or notice and investigate the noncompletion.

Creating Reinforcements

Creating reinforcement is developing ways of supporting parishioners' decisions to carry out their programs. There are three categories of reinforcements: rewards, punishments, and reminders. Rewards are pleasurable experiences that happen when one does the desired thing. Punishments are unpleasant experiences that result from not doing the desired thing. Reminders are experiences that help parishioners remember to do the desired thing. Rewards are generally more effective than punishments, and they build up parishioners' bonds with pastors. People learn to dislike the persons who punish them.

Reinforcements are necessary because people generally find it difficult to adopt new behaviors due to the pain of change, the power of habit, and the benefits provided by the old behaviors. Therefore we need support to endure the pain, resist the power, and forgo the benefits.

Like goals and program steps, reinforcements must be measurable, meaningful, and manageable. They are scheduled into the program in the same way steps are.

The most powerful of the rewards is social support—a person (or persons) notices and responds to the behavior. Likewise, the withdrawal of approval or the communication of the lack of support is a strong punishment. An example of the power of social support is the strong effect that a teenager's peer group has on his or her dress, speech, activities, and behavior. Thus it is very important to involve another person, persons, or group in supporting participation in a difficult program. A practice group providing a regular opportunity to reflect feelings and to get feedback on one's progress would be a helpful reinforcement.

An important form of reminder is monitoring. Monitoring is regular evaluation of progress in carrying out the program. The parishioner's awareness of how he or she is doing in implementing the program is a powerful form of reinforcement. Two very effective ways of monitoring are daily prayers and regular journal keeping. By incorporating petitions, thanksgivings, and confessions related to carrying out the program in daily prayers, progress can be effectively monitored. Making regular written notations about the program in a journal is similarly effective. When monitoring is done with another or others the weight of social support is added to that of awareness to make a very powerful reinforcement. If a practice group expects a report on how much one has practiced between meetings at each meeting, then monitoring is combined with social support.

Celebration, giving thanks at the end of the program, is a third type of monitoring. It gives the parishioner an opportunity to affirm the learning and changes that resulted from doing the program. It is very important to celebrate the small changes in behavior and simple lessons learned that come from participating in the program. As Bonhoeffer (1954, 29) noted, "Only he [or she] who gives thanks for the little things receives the big things." It is even important to celebrate discovering the parts of the program that are ineffectual because the knowledge of what did not work is important information for use in the planning of future programs. Thus the person who is working on doubling the times he or she reflects feelings in pastoral conversations could schedule a celebration at the end of the semester confident that there would be something to celebrate.

Types of Programs

There are three types of programs: simple overt behavioral, simple covert behavioral, and complex. The simple overt behavioral type consists of programs that are limited to dealing with action. An example of this first type is the student's plan to double the times he or she reflected feelings. The simple covert behavioral program focuses on changing thoughts. Giving thanks each day for the things one has accomplished, as a way of disputing the irrational beliefs of high self-expectations and need for perfection, is a standard program of the second category. The complex program works on both overt and covert behavior. The student who is working on improving responding skills might need to practice giving thanks so that progress might not be stopped by perfectionistic anxiety and procrastination. Giving thanks would also help the student accept and enjoy positive feedback from the practice group.

The type of program and the amount of detail needed varies according to two factors: the parishioner's need, and the difficulty of the goal. The plan need only be detailed enough to get the job done—too little detail leaves the person at sea, too much overwhelms. The evaluations of progress will indicate whether more or less detail and complexity are needed. Even the simplest programs, however, have some form of steps, schedule, and reinforcements.

PLANNING IMPLEMENTATION

Planning implementation is preparing to carry out the program. This includes reviewing the program, and, if necessary, rehearsing and revising it. Because change is so difficult, developing a program is not enough; there need to be plans for carrying it out.

Reviewing

The first step is *reviewing* the program. Reviewing consists of going over the contents of a program after it has been developed. Because parishioners are the ones who implement the programs, they are the ones who have to remember them. Thus, pastors should ask parishioners to restate in detail the program they intend to follow.

One of the ways that anxiety about change thwarts the carrying out of action plans is that it causes parishioners to forget the plan. Therefore, when the programs are long or detailed at all, pastors should invite parishioners to write them down. Reviewing then consists of having them read and explain their notes.

Reviewing both ascertains what parishioners remember and reinforces plans in their memories. It provides pastors and parishioners with opportunities to notice what parts of the plans are forgotten. What is forgotten is a cue to what causes parishioners difficulty. Therefore, reviewing gives an indication about what part of the program needs to be explored, rehearsed, or revised.

Rehearsing

Rehearsing is practicing for implementation. A key method for breaking through the anxiety about doing a program is to rehearse the steps. Rehearsal allows you to practice in a less threatening situation until you are ready for the actual situation. These practices may involve such activities as planning how you will do each step, visualizing doing them, and role playing. Rehearsing reinforces the steps in parishioners' minds and bodies. One of the steps that Rosita Sanchez had to take in her job-hunting program was to go for interviews. She was frightened at this prospect. Her pastor, Rev. Hector Ramirez, role-played the interviewer over and over until Rosita felt more confident about her ability to handle the questions.

Rehearsals show what parishioners know and need to know about the program. Often aspects of the program that seem clear in discussion become less clear when you are trying to do them; parishioners find out what they need to know. Conversely, rehearsing frequently reveals strengths; parishioners find out that they know how to do some things that they thought they did not know how to do. For example, during the rehearsal Rosita discovered that she was far more conversant in English than she had imagined. She did find that she needed to memorize more information to fill out the applications.

Rehearsals show, also, what parts of the program need revision. As parishioners talk through, walk through, or visualize the steps, they sometimes discover that steps or substeps are missing, or they may see that certain steps need to be changed. Either way, they discover the need for revision.

Revising

Revising is changing the program in order to improve its implementation. The processes of reviewing and rehearsing the steps often bring up the need for revision by indicating what is missing, difficult, or redundant in the individual steps or the whole program. Sometimes reviewing and rehearsing show that a program is too ambitious for the parishioner to carry out within her or his limits of time, talent, training, or treasure. It is important to revise the steps so that they are easy to carry out, because success in carrying out a step reinforces a parishioner's participation in the program.

Reviewing, rehearsing, and revising programs are three ways of making them more concrete and therefore more likely to be implemented. They are also the major components of the follow-up conversations that take place while persons are implementing their action plans.

CHARACTERISTICS
OF UNHELPFUL GUIDANCE

The four characteristics of unhelpful guidance are poor timing, focusing on the plan, supporting inappropriately, and neglecting specificity. Each of these characteristics combines disregard of the principles "The Holy Spirit is the guide" or "Creaturehood and sinfulness make change difficult" with slighting at least one of the facilitative conditions.

Poor Timing

Poor timing is moving too quickly or too slowly. It is tempting to push parishioners to come up with goals, programs, and implementation plans too quickly, in order to give pastors and parishioners the feeling that they have gotten something done. What is sacrificed by haste is the time to focus on the Holy Spirit as the guide. The neglected facilitative condition is empathy—pastors do not take time to help parishioners explore their feelings and thoughts about the various aspects of their action plan. This neglect of the Holy Spirit and empathy will usually result in parishioners having problems in carrying out the plan.

Conversely, parishioners will sometimes resist change by moving very, very slowly in coming up with one or more aspects of an action plan. This usually means that they are afraid to rely on the Holy Spirit's guidance, and are therefore afraid to move. In these cases pastors should help them explore their fears and understand how their perspectives contribute to their lack of trust.

Focusing on the Plan

It is easy for pastors to slip into focusing on the development of action plans to the exclusion of paying attention to parishioners' experiences of the process. This happens because pastors and parishioners find it more satisfying to deal with the mechanics of planning than with often troublesome emotions. It happens, also, because pastors or parishioners want to get something done quickly. As with poor timing, discussed above, the principle being neglected is listening to the Holy Spirit as guide and the facilitative condition being ignored is empathy.

Inappropriate Support

Pastors often find themselves taking responsibility for the implementation of action plans. Sometimes they take responsibility away from parishioners because they are too anxious to allow parishioners the freedom to fail or succeed. Other times pastors take on parishioners' responsibilities to avoid the discomfort of confronting them. Either way, parishioners are not supported appropriately because pastors are not trusting the Holy Spirit as the guide and therefore take over themselves, and thus are not showing respect and genuineness by communicating conditional regard and their true reactions.

Lack of Specificity

This is a common problem in guidance because many pastors are either not familiar with or not comfortable with the level of specificity required in setting goals, developing programs, and planning implementation. Thus they allow parishioners to develop action plans with vague objectives, incomplete programs, or inadequate support for implementation. This error is based on ignorance of either the theological principle that "creaturehood and sinfulness make change difficult" or the key facilitative condition for the guidance skills—concreteness. Concreteness gives parishioners clear ways to fight through the fog that anxiety about change brings on.

LEARNING THE SKILLS

The objective of stage 3 for parishioners is to plan and carry out an action plan designed to get them from where they are to the place they want to be. Pastors use the guidance skills of setting goals, developing programs, and planning implementation to help parishioners meet this objective. They use these skills in full knowledge that the Holy Spirit is the guide and that resistance, finiteness, and sin make change difficult. Skilled pastors' styles are governed by the facilitative conditions, especially concreteness, which is the key for the guidance skills.

Process

The purpose of the entire three-stage process is action. Thus stage 3 is the culmination. However, it is more than the goal and completion of the pastoral conversation process. Because the three-stage model continually recycles—acting leads to the exploring of new issues, leading to new understanding, then leading to further action programs—stage 3 is not just an end. It is also a beginning.

Exercises

1. *Examining Your Own Attempts to Change Behavior*

Describe a personal problem that you have been working on. Note the plans to solve it that have fit to some extent and those that have not. Then answer the following questions: What were the chief differences between these two types of plans? What were the differences in your feelings when you first considered these plans? What are some of the ways you have opposed the change that you want? What purpose(s) did this opposition serve? What events and thoughts cue the behavior you were trying to change? What feelings, experiences (especially social support), actions, and thoughts reinforced the behavior you were trying to change?

2. *Developing an Action Plan*

Take the problem, such as the one described in the previous exercises, and set a goal for managing that problem or some significant aspect of it. Then develop a program to reach that goal—including steps, sequencing, and reinforcements. Finally, plan implementation by reviewing, rehearsing, and revising it with a skilled pastor.

3. *Practicing Guidance in a Practice Group*

Begin with a parishioner who brings a problem or joy that he or she has explored and understood. The parishioner should be ready to develop an action plan. This readiness is the key to this exercise being successful. After using stage 1 skills to gain an understanding of the problem or joy, the pastor endeavors to guide the parishioner in setting goals, developing programs, and planning implementation. Then an observer(s) debriefs the pastor and parishioner about the process and concludes by offering his or her observations.

CONCLUSION

The Metanoia Model

THE METANOIA MODEL derives its name from the Greek word *metanoia,* which means to change one's mind or attitude. This word reflects the basic thesis of the model: the way to help persons deal with their problems is to help them change the beliefs that contribute to their distressing feelings and behaviors. Thus, the goal of the model is to help people change through hearing and responding to the gospel.

The model integrates three types of pastoral skills to accomplish this goal: helping skills, theological assessment, and religious resources. The helping skills provide the three-stage (exploring, understanding, acting) organization of the model. They also provide the specific techniques of presence, proclamation, and guidance. Theological assessment is the process of identifying the unhelpful beliefs that lie behind problem feelings and behaviors. This assessment gives direction to the model: the presence skills are used to identify the beliefs, proclamation disputes the unhelpful beliefs, and guidance helps parishioners set up plans to continue the disputation by word and deed. Such religious resources as pastoral persons, Scripture, tradition, contemporary theology and ethics, covenant communities, prayer, and rites are pastors' unique tools for disputing the unhelpful ideas and teaching the gospel. The helping skills, theological assessment, and religious resources are all used by pastors to help draw out, identify, and support the insights and directions that the Holy Spirit communicates directly to parishioners. The metanoia model is a problem-solving (or problem management) construct that is appropriate for both the very brief counseling (1–6 weekly sessions) on a specific issue, which characterizes the majority of pastoral contacts, and the limited training of nonspecialist pastors. With this overview of the metanoia model we can now turn to a stage-by-stage review.

STAGE 1: EXPLORING

The first task of parishioners is to explore where they are in relation to the issue at hand. They do this by considering the feelings, experiences, actions, and thoughts they have regarding the issue. Pastors use presence skills of attending, responding, and assessing to help parishioners do this task.

Attending is paying attention to parishioners by positioning, observing their nonverbals, and listening to both their words and manner of speaking. Attending has benefits for pastors and parishioners: it helps parishioners get involved in the process by communicating pastors' interest in them and it is the source of data for pastors.

Responding is communicating what pastors have seen and heard and inviting further exploration by paraphrasing and probing. Paraphrasing is restating in pastors' own words the core of parishioners' statements; it helps parishioners by inviting them to say more and letting them rehear what they have already said. Probing or asking questions assists parishioners to expand their replies or make them more specific. Both responding skills are aids to exploration. They also deepen pastors' understanding of parishioners' feelings, experiences, actions, and thoughts.

Assessing is detecting the beliefs that contribute to parishioners' key feelings and actions about their issues through summarizing, hunching, and eliciting. Summarizing pulls together the data gathered through attending and responding. Hunching expresses guesses about the beliefs that are implied in parishioners' stories. Eliciting, the third skill, uses probes to draw out parishioners' beliefs. These assessing skills help parishioners explore their issues at a new depth, as well as deepen pastors' understanding.

STAGE 1 SUMMARY CHART

PRESENCE	Attending	positioning observing listening
	Responding	paraphrasing probing
	Assessing	summarizing hunching eliciting
Enables		
EXPLORING		feelings, experiences, actions, and thoughts

STAGE 2: UNDERSTANDING

Parishioners' stage 2 task is understanding how the gospel disputes their unhelpful beliefs that contribute to despair, dread, and alienation; and affirms their liberating beliefs that support acceptance, hope, and love. After pastors have categorized parishioners' beliefs theologically, they use one or more of the proclamation skills of informing, sharing, confronting, and contending to challenge the unhelpful beliefs and communicate the good news. They then use the responding skills and reviewing to help parishioners explore and understand their proclamations.

Informing, sharing, confronting, contending, and reviewing are five different ways of challenging unhelpful beliefs and affirming the good news. Informing communicates information, sharing offers pastors' experiences, confronting exposes differences in perception between pastor and parishioners, and contending disputes beliefs with reason and religious resources. Each is designed to help parishioners understand the weaknesses of the unhelpful beliefs and the power of the good news. They are all assertive ways to tell the gospel story effectively. Reviewing invites parishioners to summarize their understanding of pastors' proclamations.

STAGE 2 SUMMARY CHART

PROCLAMATION	Informing, sharing, confronting, contending, and reviewing
Enables	
UNDERSTANDING	the gospel message that conquers despair, dread, and alienation

STAGE 3: ACTING

After parishioners have understood the good news, their task is to develop an action plan to get them from where they are to where they want to be. Pastors aid parishioners in this task through the guidance skills of setting goals, developing programs, and planning implementation. Many action plans include the religious resources: pastoral persons, Scripture, tradition, theology and ethics, covenant communities, prayer and the arts, and rites. These tools help parishioners dispute the unhelpful beliefs and incorporate the good news in their lives.

The three guidance skills are setting goals, developing programs, and planning implementation. Setting goals involves moving from vague intents and general goals to concrete objectives that are meaningful, measurable, and manageable. Developing programs includes choosing steps, scheduling them, and then creating reinforcements to support the resolve to take the steps. After the programs are designed, parishioners prepare to carry them out by planning implementation through reviewing, rehearsing, and revising.

STAGE 3 SUMMARY CHART

GUIDANCE	Setting Goals	vague intent
		general goal
		concrete objective
	Developing Programs	choosing steps
		sequencing steps
		creating reinforce-
		ments
	Planning Implementation	reviewing
		rehearsing
		revising

Each of these clusters of skills is employed in a different way. Usually all of the presence skills are used during most conversations. Attending and responding are done at the same time, whereas assessing comes after considerable attending and responding. The proclamation skills are different because only one is always used—reviewing. Pastors have to choose which of the others they will utilize in their challenges. The guidance skills and subskills are used in strict order because each one builds on the previous one.

VARYING TIME AND DEPTH

The metanoia model can be used in the full range of pastoral care from brief conversations at the door to multisession counseling, as illustrated by the varied examples throughout this book. The main difference between the types of conversations is the amount of *time and depth* at each stage. In the brief conversations much of the time is devoted to a quickly defined stage 1 followed by a stage 2 that consists of a brief comment or two by the pastor, and then a stage 3 in which the pastor and parishioner agree on a simple plan. The example using a conflict over the new prayer book in chapter 2 is an example of this brief type. The longer conversations are characterized by more depth and dialogue in stages 1 and 2 and a detailed plan in stage 3. The supervisory conversation that leads off chapters 5 and 7 is an example of a longer conversation. Theological assessments guide pastors in both types of conversation, but in the brief conversations pastors often share the results of their assessments without making them explicit to parishioners, as was the case in the conflict over the new prayer book. Likewise, the use of religious resources (other than the pastor) is less extensive in the brief conversations.

In sum, the metanoia model is a three-stage construction for pastoral conversations that is designed to assist persons to become skilled pastors. It does this by providing structure and guidance that help pastors to be adept at using helping skills, theological assessment, and religious resources to communicate the gospel to parishioners.

Bibliography

.

Bonhoeffer, D. 1954. *Life Together.* Trans. John W. Doberstein. San Francisco: Harper & Row.

Carkhuff, R. R. 1983. *The Art of Helping.* 5th ed. Amherst, Mass.: Human Resources Development Press.

————. 1969. *Helping and Human Relations.* 2 vols. Amherst, Mass.: Human Resources Development Press.

Carkhuff, R. R., and W. Anthony. 1979. *The Skills of Helping.* Amherst, Mass.: Human Resources Development Press.

Carrington, P. 1982. Meditation Techniques in Clinical Practice. In *The Newer Therapies: A Sourcebook,* ed. L. E. Abt and Irving R. Stuart, 60–78. New York: D. Van Nostrand.

Cavanagh, M. E. 1982. *The Counseling Experience.* Monterey, Calif.: Brooks/ Cole.

Clinebell, H. 1981. *Contemporary Growth Therapies.* Nashville: Abingdon.

Condon, J. C., and F. S. Yousef. 1975. *An Introduction to Intercultural Communication.* New York: Macmillan.

Daly, M. J., and R. L. Burton. 1983. Self-Esteem and Irrational Beliefs. *Journal of Counseling Psychology* 30:361–66.

Egan, G. 1982. *The Skilled Helper.* 2d ed. Monterey, Calif.: Brooks/Cole.

Ellis, A. 1974. *Humanistic Psychotherapy.* New York: McGraw-Hill.

————. 1971. *Growth Through Reason.* Palo Alto, Calif.: Science and Behavior Books.

————. 1977. Rational-emotive therapy: Research data that supports the clinical and personality hypothesis of RET and other modes of cognitive behavior therapy. *The Counseling Psychologist* 7:2–42.

————. 1962. *Reason and Emotion in Psychotherapy.* New York: Lyle Stuart.

Ellis, A., and R. A. Harper. *A New Guide to Rational Living.* North Hollywood, Calif.: Wilshire.

Frank, J. D. 1974. *Persuasion and Healing.* Rev. ed. New York: Schocken.

Garland, D. S. R., and D. E. Garland. 1986. *Beyond Companionship: Christians in Marriage.* Philadelphia: Westminster.

Gaylin, W. 1979. *Feelings: Our Vital Signs.* San Francisco: Harper & Row.

Grieger, R., and J. Boyd. 1980. *Rational-Emotive Therapy.* New York: D. Van Nostrand.

Gurman, A. S., and A. W. Razin. 1977. *Effective Psychotherapy: A Handbook of Research.* New York: Pergamon.

Hammond, D., D. H. Hepworth, and V. G. Smith. 1977. *Improving Therapeutic Communication.* San Francisco: Jossey-Bass.

Hauck, P. A. 1973. *Overcoming Depression.* Philadelphia: Westminster.

———. 1974. *Overcoming Frustration and Anger.* Philadelphia: Westminster.

———. 1975. *Overcoming Worry and Fear.* Philadelphia: Westminster.

Jacobs, M. 1985. *Swift to Hear: Facilitating Skills in Listening and Responding.* London: SPCK.

Jones, R. C. 1968. A Factored Measure of Ellis' Irrational Belief System with Personality and Maladjustment Correlations. Ph.D. diss., Texas Tech University, 1968. *Dissertation Abstracts* 29:4379A–80A.

Oden, T. C. 1969. *The Structure of Awareness.* Nashville: Abingdon.

Rogers, C. 1961. *On Becoming a Person.* New York: Houghton Mifflin.

Truax, C. B., and R. R. Carkhuff. 1967. *Toward Effective Counseling and Psychotherapy.* Chicago: Aldine.

Virkler, H. A. 1980. The Facilitativeness of Parish Ministers. *Journal of Psychology and Theology* 8:140–46.

Ward, J. N. 1983. Contemplation. In *The Westminster Dictionary of Christian Spirituality,* ed. G. S. Wakefield, 95–96. Philadelphia: Westminster.

Zwemer, W. A., and J. L. Deffenbacher. 1984. Irrational Beliefs, Anger, and Anxiety. *Journal of Counseling Psychology* 31:391–93.